CREATIVELY Productive

"Lisa presents us a remarkable gift wrapped in alliteration and authenticity, vulnerability and hard truths. Part memoir, part how-to manual, and part pure magic, we learn how to put ourselves, our students, and our loved ones in a better place to succeed—simply by approaching our day-to-day learning experiences with more intention, more purpose, and substantially more whimsy. Lisa doesn't just suggest these ideals, she embodies them—and thus we can place ourselves in her capable words."

—**Dan Ryder**, education director, Success & Innovation
Center at Mt. Blue Campus, Farmington, ME

"This is more than a book; it is a guide you can dive back into whenever you need support, redirection, refocus, and ideas. Lisa has beautifully shared and inspires you to take your note-taking, organization, planning, and reflection to an entirely new level. Each section leaves you inspired and reflecting along with some great starting points of best practice with your learners. This book is like a good hug—something you'll go back to because it just feels that good."

—**Tami Brewster**, elementary generalist,
English Montreal School Board

"*Creatively Productive* is energized calmness. It offers readers a joy-filled journey into a more organized life that celebrates purpose and prioritizes customized processes and reflection. Through stories from the classroom and explored ideas from her own questions and adventures in learning and in life, Lisa invites educators to be curious, creative, and connected. Packed with practical tips, detailed steps for implementation, and ready-to-explore templates, *Creatively Productive* is a great addition for any educator's book shelf!"

—**Dr. Jennifer Williams**, education strategist at Participate;
professor, Saint Leo University, Clearwater, FL

"This is a must-have book for any educator or individual who seeks to better their craft or their quality of life! Lisa Johnson does a superb job of providing rich resources, relevant examples, and creative ideas on how to effectively use technology to establish order out of the chaos in one's life. The duality of this book allows educators to teach their students necessary organizational skills using technology, and it can provide individuals a process for individual reflection and self-improvement in a unique and interesting way."

—**Vickie Bauerle**, retired principal and clinical
assistant professor, University of Texas, Austin, TX

"Lisa's enthusiasm for being productive in the most creative way possible shines through in this book. *Creatively Productive* is full of ideas, examples, and most importantly, inspiration. In particular, I love the convergence of digital and analog technology and the recognition that there is more than one 'correct' path on the road to being successful."

—**Julie Willcott**, educator, Kennebec Valley
Community College, Fairfield, ME

"I've been a fan of Lisa Johnson's work since I discovered her Instagram account a year ago. Her creative note-taking and colorful organization ideas have inspired me to be more intentional in this area. In a day and age where distractions are at an all-time high, *Creatively Productive* unlocks the secrets of tackling the time wasters and clutter in our busy lives. Full of practical examples, eye-catching photos, and ingenious ideas, this book will be an invaluable resource for students, educators, parents, writers, and creatives!"

—**Julie Campbell**, award-winning journalist
and freelance writer, Indianapolis, IN

"Lisa does an outstanding job of providing useful and timely information on being productive. If you are looking for effective ways to organize yourself or your students, Lisa provides a plethora of ideas that are both digital and analog. This book is a must-have to help readers understand the greatness of being organized in all avenues of life."

—**Andrea Keller**, middle school librarian,
Lamar Middle School, Irving, TX

"I love the conversational style in Lisa's writing. With all of the pop culture linking and references, I found myself LOL-ing or saying, 'Right?!' The end of each chapter has how-to application of its content. Every teacher or instructional coach should own this book."

—**Erin Barnes**, principal, Epic Charter School, Tulsa, OK

"*Creatively Productive* is a fabulous book that provides educators with everything they need to help students be successful. With heart and humor, Lisa Johnson has captured the importance of teaching students that staying organized is essential to being successful in class as well as in life. From note-taking to calendaring, bullet journaling to sketch-noting, Lisa shares tons of powerful, impactful strategies and digital tools that take organization to the next level."

—**Charlotte Dolat**, instructional coach,
Alamo Heights High School, San Antonio, TX

"Wow! *Creatively Productive* is an idea-filled book on topics such as goal-setting, organization, productivity, habit-tracking, positive procrastination, and so much more. There are immediate takeaways for students, teachers, and anyone looking to hone their time and organizational skills. Lisa Johnson offers visual examples as well as core content connections that teachers can use with their students right away."

—**Becky Calzada**, library services coordinator, Leander ISD, Leander, TX

"Lisa Johnson's new book places emphasis on the transferable skills that are essential for students of all ages. If you follow Lisa on social media or have heard her speak, you already know her passion for bullet journaling and finding a balance between analog and digital. In *Creatively Productive,* you'll learn actionable information and find resources to push your thinking as an educator!"

—**Monica Burns**, EdTech and curriculum consultant,
Class Tech Tips, LLC, Jersey City, NJ

"Feeling overwhelmed and struggling to keep your life organized? How do you think your students are responding to the heavy demands that are placed upon them? The scary question is, *are we modeling best preparation practices for the learners we serve?*

"Fear not. *Creatively Productive* provides solutions in abundance! Within this gem, Lisa Johnson shares practical strategies and innovative applications to teach all learners to "clear the clutter" of life while finding joy in the process. You will also glean insight to tackle those time wasters that threaten to zap your productive potential every single day.

"For what are you waiting? The wisdom penned by Lisa is sure to inspire and motivate you to change your day-to-day practices (and that of your students) and become creatively productive!"

—Tara Martin, educator, author, keynote speaker,
Dave Burgess Consulting, Inc. director of marketing
and communications, DBC, Inc., Lawrence, KS

"In *Creatively Productive*, Lisa walks the reader through multiple meaningful and purposeful strategies and tools that can be implemented in the classroom right away. No two students learn exactly the same way, and Lisa offers many practical suggestions to guide students to be successful no matter the project or assignment."

—Kayla Delzer, North Dakota teacher of the year; CEO;
globally awarded teacher, Top Dog Teaching, Inc., Fargo, ND

"Lisa Johnson provides an accessible and authentic framework for tackling the rabbit hole of our over-scheduled and over-informed lives by offering manageable and realistic best practices. Grab a highlighter and your Apple ID—it's time to organize the chaos!"

—Brianna Hodges, EdTech coordinator, Eanes ISD, Austin, TX

"Keeping your house in order can be a difficult task. Throw a 'digital house' into the mix, and the idea can seem herculean. Lisa provides a practical, no-nonsense, and real-world application to life/data management and does it in a way that is fun and engaging and embraces both digital and analog means. Students and adults alike can benefit from her ideas!"

—Lucas Loughmiller, director of library and instructional
media services, Manhattan-Ogden USD 383, Manhattan, KS

CREATIVELY Productive

Essential Skills for Tackling Time Wasters, Clearing the Clutter, and Succeeding in School—and Life!

Lisa Johnson

CREATIVELY PRODUCTIVE

© 2019 by Lisa Johnson

This book is available at special discounts when purchased in quantity for use as premiums, promotions, fundraisers, or for educational use. For inquiries and details, contact the publisher at books@daveburgessconsulting.com.

Published by Dave Burgess Consulting, Inc.
San Diego, CA
DaveBurgessConsulting.com

Cover Design by Genesis Kohler
Editing and Interior Design by My Writers' Connection

Library of Congress Control Number: 2018965583
Paperback ISBN: 978-1-949595-08-6
Ebook ISBN: 978-1-949595-09-3

First Printing: January 2019

Dedication

To my boys, Hayden and Gavin . . .

My hope for you is that you will find passion and purpose in the perennial and hold on to what matters most in this fast-paced world.

Contents

Beware the Jabberwocky
(and Other Obstacles That
Threaten to Slow You Down)

Beyond the world of daily curriculum lies a hidden realm, one that deeply impacts students but that too often we miss or don't have time to explore with them. *Creatively Productive* is intended to help you discover this realm and unlock its secrets through a variety of challenges. You might be wondering why the jabberwocky gets a mention here, as he is a small blip in the *Alice in Wonderland* story. Though a grim poem, the jabberwocky represents the obstacles we must navigate and overcome. The obstacles you and your learners encounter might include digital clutter, time management, missed opportunities, or unmet goals.

Alice spends much of her time in her story wandering in a dream-like state of curiosity, fantasy, and whimsy. That's one reason I love *Alice in Wonderland*, and while I hope to appeal to your passions and emotions with the tools and ideas I share in this book, I am keenly aware that the real world and school life are not dream-like. We have much to accomplish on any given day, which is why I hope to appeal to your sense of reality and reason as much as to your sense of wonder. It's why I toe the line between whimsy and wisdom in hopes of helping you see how these timeless tools and tactics are good for you and your students. Whimsy makes things fun and interesting; wisdom grounds the whimsy and helps us make sense of the chaos that surrounds us. In truth, we need both, like salt and pepper or perhaps sweet and savory. And with the Wakeful Whimsy activities at the end of each chapter and the Working Wisdoms found at the end of the book, you'll get plenty of each.

- **Wakeful Whimsy:** If you look up the word wakeful, you will see the definition "carefully observant or attentive" or "marked by full consciousness or alertness."[1] True whimsy feels ethereal, almost like you are floating. Wakeful whimsy adds a layer of purpose. It tethers us to the now. It allows us to be creative and explore flights of fancy with our eyes open. The Wakeful Whimsy activities are intended to be more illustrious and creative, but they are still grounded in purpose and direction. These are included at the end of each chapter.

- **Working Wisdoms:** These are found at the end of the book. Multiple definitions exist for "working," and I chose to exploit them all. Working Wisdoms are ideas that work from people who work. They are intended to create a springboard for you and your students. As my intent for this book is to create a future-ready resource, I sought to discover the wisdom in a variety of careers. I wanted to know what people in the "real world" think and experience. The Working Wisdoms can be digested as an aperitif or dessert. They are not included in the text itself but do play into the book's wisdom; additionally, insights from myself as well as fellow authors and people in the industry are great to use with students or as a starting point for further research.

Before I tell you what this book is, I should tell you what it isn't. The book is not intended to be a scholastic play-by-play although there are many practical strategies and processes included. It is not meant to be a tool to raise your test scores or improve a student's GPA for the next year or six although it does include many tips that will help students learn more effectively. This book is designed like a Wikipedia on steroids to give you an overview of many topics that will propel you to other places to dig into each more deeply. Finally, it is not a tool to ace a class; rather, it is a collection of resources curated to help you and your learners ace *life*.

Each of the next six chapters focuses on one set of skills. We'll look first at the need for and/or importance of each skill and then explore specific strategies you can use to foster and grow these competencies:

Chapter 1: Calming the Chaos—Tips for using portfolios, archiving student work, and ultimately devising and adopting an individual plan for organization

Chapter 2: Taming Time—An introduction to a variety of calendar, planner, and bullet journal tools as well as strategies for breaking down tasks, proactively managing time, and limiting distractions

Chapter 3: Notes on Note-Taking—An overview of four different note-taking styles, strategies for curating information and content, tips for before, after, and during lectures, and some ideas for personal note-taking and blending analog and digital notes

Chapter 4: Goal Setting and Habit Tracking—A guide to determining values, setting visible goals, creating and tracking habits, and avoiding procrastination

Chapter 5: The Power of Reflection—Ideas for student reflections (personal and academic)

Chapter 6: Read, Write, Review—Surprisingly educational reads, ideas for reading retention and reader's notebooks, plus additional suggestions for a learner's notebook

Now to what the book is. As to the rest of the book's design, content, and purpose, I have divided that into the following six sections:

Double Duty

The purpose of this book is to illuminate the hidden skills students need to be successful and provide multiple pathways to guide students through these skills. Whether you are an education technologist (EdTech), a librarian, a curriculum specialist, a principal, or a classroom teacher, the tools and strategies you'll find here are for you to use as you support teachers or as you work directly with students. Unlike books that are designed to teach vocabulary and/or long division that are ultimately for you to adopt practices to use with and for your students, this book seeks to offer a duality. Lewis Carroll states in the prologue for *Through the Looking Glass*, "We are bit older children, dear." [2] Simple. Profound. True. And as such, everything in this book can be adapted and adopted for your own professional and personal life. But with the duality, I hope there is purpose. Teachers aren't just teachers in the classroom . . . they don't shed their teacher suit (or human one) when they go home. My hope is that you explore and adopt these practices in a way that you can share authentic experiences with what works and does not work for you with your students and colleagues.

Perennial and Practical

Intrigued with some of the ideas and practices I was sharing online for organization, journaling, and time management, a dear friend asked if she could use them at her daughter's school. I happily obliged. Two of the questions she asked teachers in her training really spoke to me [3]:

- "Who is at the heart of your work when thinking about organization, journaling, note-taking, and list making?"
- "Who can benefit?"

Too often districts purchase an idea and/or fabricate a vision and pass it on to teachers to disseminate to students. Perhaps it is a buzzword. Perhaps it is a philosophy. This kind of vision fizzles out quickly because these buzzwords and philosophies have no passion and typically lack practicality. In this book, it is my goal to provide perennial and practical resources about which you can be passionate for yourself and your students for years and years to come.

I am really fascinated with analog and nostalgia. Particularly the ideas, tools, and practices that straddle nostalgia and perennial. I am exceptionally curious about what makes something perennial and why certain tools and practices seem to always get a second life. I also love pop culture, and I would like to think I have always been an observer of the world. I tend to notice dots and connect them in my head. A few dots I have been noticing lately are nostalgia and analog. I can't say if it is the explosion of content on the internet or just the cycle of time, but nostalgia is running rampant from a return to coloring books to rebooted shows and movies like *Gilmore Girls, Roseanne, Fuller House, Chips, Teenage Mutant Ninja Turtles, My Little Pony,* and *Transformers,* to name a few. And let's not forget recent documentaries on the beloved Mr. Rogers or iconic *Highlights* magazine. Analog is making a comeback too (or perhaps it is just staying strong):

- **Books:** Many people still read and prefer actual paper books—I am one of them. While Borders may be out of business, I must tell you that places like public libraries and private sellers like Barnes and Noble, Amazon, and Half Price Books are still thriving. And don't even get me started on record players, card catalogs, typewriters, Dr. Martens, and vintage books.

- **Planners:** But wait, there's more. People who scrapped their paper planners for Google Calendar are now returning to their old ways . . . to a degree. It should be stated that they haven't exactly scrapped Google Calendar, but they find that both a paper planner and a digital one seem to work in symbiosis. It should also be noted that in my last eight years as an EdTech, staff never received a paper planner—until this year. And I practically got a standing ovation at a principals' meeting when I designed a paper monthly calendar that included the dates of each professional development (PD) session we were to offer over the summer.

- **Whiteboards:** Another interesting trend I have witnessed is the whiteboard phenomenon. Rather than every room having a SMARTBoard, more and more classrooms and spaces are simply adding a projector and then opting for whiteboards, glass boards, or writable walls. With all the productivity and project management tools that exist, I still see whiteboards used in almost every office for planning and long-term projects.

- **Notes:** I have worked in an instructional support role with students since the beginning of the iPad. I have witnessed the paperless trend, and I have also seen interesting resurgences. Yes, many of our students do take notes in classes digitally with their iPad, but many students will ask for a paper handout or packet over a digital one. I also see many students taking notes in analog with their "ROYGBIV'd" PaperMate® Flairs® and sticky notes. And for some unknown reason, we seem to be printing and copying more paper than in years past.

In the wake of the explosion of technology and information over the past ten to twenty years, what constants have stood the test of time in your life? What kinds of activities and tools have returned or rebooted? Answering these questions isn't exactly like a crystal ball for the future, but it does help us see how combining the old and new can create systems and tools that work better than either on its own. I do want to make a clear distinction: This book is not a call to return to analog. If that were the case, you could simply pick up any book that was written on these topics over the past two decades. What sets this book apart from those is that it is intended to be both a thorough love letter to the perennial and a guidebook for the future. Like many of you, I personally rode the wave of analog to digital. Today I reside on the shore of a secondary high school and witness the needs of students daily. To write about the future, you must live and observe the present—that is what this book seeks to achieve.

In the same vein of perennial, when Yolanda Barker and I wrote and published the professional development iBook of higher-order thinking skills, *Hot Apps 4 Hots*, we deliberately used a cooking theme. We did this because we wanted to remain content neutral. We knew if we developed a seventh-grade pre-algebra lesson using the Talking Tom app, teachers who didn't teach seventh grade math would tune out that app even though it could be used in a variety of other ways in pretty much any content area and grade level. My hope for this book, just like the iBook, was to create a resource that everyone could chew on and digest—a resource that tackled issues and met needs that educators and students faced daily. I wanted to create a resource that met the needs of many without diluting content or focus and yet at the same time allowed for multiple recipes to be created once you had a handle on the ingredients. I wanted to create a book of ingredients with which anyone could cook.

Timeless and Techy

Sometimes I feel like a walking contradiction. I'm an EdTech who teaches soft skills, an English teacher who taught math, a people pleaser who seeks out-of-the-box ideas and doesn't like following directions, and someone with ADD that is organized. That said, I don't want you to feel the disequilibrium one experiences when tumbling down a rabbit hole unexpectedly, so I feel like I must, for two reasons, connect the dots: first, to connect the dots of my journey to write this book and then to connect the dots of why all these things are so important now—perhaps now more than ever. If you've read my blog *TechChef4u*, you might think this blending of analog and digital contradicts its message. But if you go back even as far as three or four years ago in my blogs, you will see I talk about blending analog and digital even then. Some years ago, I attended a Women in Leadership conference. One of the sessions focused on Polarity Thinking and that idea has stuck with me to this day. The speaker drove home her point by talking about rest and exercise, noting that they aren't opposites; they are poles. Too much rest may atrophy your muscles, and too much exercise might do you in, but exercise and rest work best in harmony.

Too often we think of trends and movements in education as opposites. Paperless classrooms are touted over paper, augmented and virtual reality over hands-on experiences. And one must wonder, *have we mixed a bit too much madness into our methodology?* Technology and analog aren't oil and water. They aren't opposites; they are poles. Try this: Draw a coordinate plane, consider these four questions and responses, and note that there are positive and negative impacts of both poles.

What are some of the good things associated with teaching in the digital realm?

- *rapid sharing, easy editing, collaboration, access to experiences students would not have in real life*

What are some of the not-so-good things associated with the digital realm?

- *headaches, distraction, cost-prohibitive tools*

What are some of the good things associated with teaching in the analog realm?

- *focus, hands-on, improved memory and retention*

What are some of the not-so-good things associated with the analog realm?

- *harder to edit, more difficult to share, kills trees*

As you can see, both analog and digital will eke out favorable and not-so-favorable results. And therein lies another duality. In 2007, the first iPhone was released, and in 2010, the iPad, and even before that, iPods were changing the face of education. As with any new trend or tool, the pendulum swung very far in the realm of digital. You don't have to be a physics major to know that what swings up or to the side will swing back in time. The pendulum will likely never swing fully back to analog, but what is probable is that we will find a healthy balance between the two. With articles like "Facebook should be regulated like cigarette industry," "Tech Backlash Grows as Investors Press Apple to Act on Children's Use," "Brain Drain: The Mere Presence of One's Own Smart Phone Reduces Available Cognitive Capacity," and "Yes, Smartphones Are Destroying a Generation, but Not of Kids," I think it is safe to say that the honeymoon with digital has expired, and we have taken off our rose-colored glasses. Please know that I am not saying this book will be disparaging the merits of technology in favor of analog. On the contrary, this book is about achieving a healthy balance or equilibrium. So I share analog and digital options, and many times I opt to focus on processes, practices, and ideas sans a tool and leave the tool open to your interpretation. My point is that we must start seeing the world in gradients. To do that, we must embrace the practices, processes, and pedagogies that are the best for our students regardless of the tools we choose to use.

Curiosity and Curations

I have always been inquisitive and had a love of research. I was that student who hassled the professor to ensure that my papers were of the caliber needed to keep my 4.0, and one professor's words helped answer that query. He told me that I would know when I was done when everything I found led to similar findings. Essentially, when I reached the bottom of the rabbit hole, I could move on. Perhaps it is my Type-A personality or these words that further fueled my need to be thorough and cast a wide and deep net anytime I decide to venture out on a knowledge quest. Who knows? And I guess it would only make sense that some of my favorite books are collections of ideas. *The Happiness Equation: Want Nothing + Do Anything = Have Everything* by Neil Pasricha and *Reinvent Yourself* by James Altucher are really just a collection of vetted ideas and personal experiences; in fact, Pasricha mentions early on in his book, "Many of these studies have been discussed in journals, conference keynotes, and research reports, but I've brought them together for you here."[4] Altucher masterfully includes more than forty essays in his book. Some are observations, and some are based on interviews. Chapters like "Einstein's Secret to Productivity," "The Ten Things I Learned from Richard Branson," "How to Get an MBA from Eminem," and "Six Things I've Learned from Mick Jagger" show how James curates clever ideas and crafts stories around them. This book, like those, is a thoughtful curation of ideas, practices, and processes I have used with my students, benefitted from myself, or observed others using. And I think the key word is "use." I would never share anything that I or someone else haven't used and/or hadn't found to be useful.

Theme and Design

As to the *Alice in Wonderland* metaphor throughout the book, I chose to script the diet version—same great taste, no filler, and no sugary, heavy-handed, forced metaphors of smoking caterpillars. I did explore a few themes and imagery. I have divided the book into two parts. Part I provides a practical foundation. It focuses on strategies and tools that are more concrete and easier to access and implement (e.g., managing digital clutter, managing time, and managing a process for note-taking). Its lessons and resources will help *shrink your problems* by minimizing digital clutter, maximizing time, and committing to practices that add an element of critical thinking to note-taking. Part II (while also practical) offers some tools and practices that will take a little longer to implement. Its purpose is to *help you grow* through exercises like goal setting, reflection, and keeping a learner's journal. If we were following a typical fairy tale plot, one would have to read the first three chapters prior to the last three. They might even be forced to navigate the rickety bridge from Part I to Part II and answer three questions from the troll hidden under said bridge. You are obviously free to read the book in a linear manner, but no chapter is really a prerequisite for another.

When I was a child, it was a standard practice in our family to Armor All my new shoes. It definitely took longer to do this than to just put them on and go, but they were protected and lasted longer. Perhaps we are not looking to raise shiny people, but the other half of that REM song equation is still valid . . . happy. We can teach students to have an impact on and in the future and to advocate for themselves if we arm them with the right tools. In true Alice fashion, this book is intended to shrink your problems and help you grow.

Because I am writing a book that has an *Alice in Wonderland* theme for educators, I thought I would play a bit with the whimsical idea of amulets or badges. An amulet is meant to protect you or offer some sort of power. And really, knowledge is power. With each chapter, I offer an amulet. For educators, this is an amulet of knowledge and experience on the topic covered in the chapter. For students, one could use the My Students Can statements as mini or micro badges for students. Each of the chapters provides an icon for the amulet which could easily be turned into a badge.

Professional and Personal

Some of this is covered in the section on theme and design, but I wanted to expand it just a bit. When I read a book, I hope the author has done two things: modeled whatever they are teaching and/or touting in the book and written the book the way they would speak or at the very least infused their personality and style. The latter is easy. I wanted to stay true to both my values and my personality. If we hung out, I would inevitably weave into our conversation a random segue or interlude/excerpt interjected from a book, show, or movie. I would most definitely mention the last book I was reading. And I doubt I could go a few days without mentioning Blue October or setting my eyes on some aqua, teal, turquoise, cyan, or cerulean object that spoke to me. The former I wove into my first book and have continued to do so with this one. As my first book focused on communication, I thought it only fitting to model those skills in my own writing, providing headers and numbered subheads so you have a clear idea of what each portion of the book will be about. I also like to include personal stories and metaphors to convey meaning and to use visuals whenever possible to provide more context and support for the text.

In real life, I am a pretty organized bullet-journal-junkie bibliophile who loves binging on Netflix, researching and curating, and jamming out to Macklemore, Twenty One Pilots, and Blue October. I am also a bit of a "word nerd" and an alliteration addict. All this to say that I could whitewash all this information and create a bland cereal with a spoonful of sterilized strategies, or I could use the ingredients that make me *me* and weave them into the recipe. As I mentioned before, I don't share ideas or practices that I don't use and/or find to be useful; likewise, I didn't want to write something that wasn't a clear reflection of my values both in the text and how the information is arranged and designed. I hope you enjoy the craft that went into this book, and I hope it inspires you to be the best version of you and to find and share your own authentic voice, as only you can do.

Audience

I realize it seems odd to mention the audience for this book at the end of the introduction rather than the beginning. Clearly, if you are reading this book, you are the audience for it; still, I encourage you to share this book with others. After all, this book is designed to support staff and students alike. And the way to do that is to share, share, share. Share the ideas you plan to use, share the topics and strategies about which you have questions, and share the successes you and your students have with these resources. As an EdTech at a high school, I realize no day is ever typical, and I end up working closely with a variety of other staff members. It is through my work and efforts with students and staff members, fellow authors, my PLN, and the greater Instagram community that I have been able to carefully curate and craft the resources detailed in the next six chapters. And these recipes become even more savory when we share and adapt them with others. Below are some groups to consider:

- **Teachers** looking to support students and/or integrate these ideas into their classroom and curriculum
- **Librarians and EdTechs** looking to support and/or design PD for staff and students
- **School Counselors, Academic Deans, or Parents** looking to support students with how to manage their digital and analog lives
- **Anyone** looking to delve into these strategies

With the backstory now illuminated, I wish you the best as you embark on your journey to slay the jabberwocky using the power of the amulets you collect along the way.

Citations

1. *The Free Dictionary.* "wakeful." TheFreeDictionary.com. 2018. thefreedictionary.com/wakeful.
2. Carroll, Lewis. *Alice's Adventures in Wonderland and Other Stories.* New York, New York: Barnes & Noble, 2010.
3. O'Clair, Audrey. "Journaling." Presentation at Maranacook Community, 2018.
4. Pasricha, Neil. *The Happiness Equation.* New York, New York: G.P. Putnam's Son, 2016.

Research

- Altucher, James. 2017. *Reinvent Yourself.* CreateSpace Independent Publishing Platform.
- Kise, Jane. "Unleashing the Positive Power of Differences." Presentation at Corwin Women in Leadership, 2016.

PART 1

Ideas to Shrink Your Problems

CHAPTER 1

Calming the Chaos

I move that the meeting adjourn, for the immediate adoption of more energetic remedies.

—Dodo, Alice's Adventures in Wonderland

Amulet: A Folder

We just met a few pages ago, and now I am going to wax intellectual with tips for you and your classroom and/ or campus. I would never do that in the real world—the real world in which I am an educational technologist and where my livelihood is built on trust, which boils down to ethos (my character and credibility), pathos (passion and emotion), and logos (reason and research). And I hope to do no differently amongst these pages. Pathos and logos are baked into each chapter, as I am passionate about organization, time management, note-taking, goal setting, journaling, and reflection, and I try to seamlessly weave in research and best practices regarding these topics throughout. So I thought it best to start with ethos. To do that, we must go back, *way* back, to get to know each other a bit.

1.1 It All Started When I Was a Wee Girl

I was an only child for four years before my brother was born. I eventually had two brothers, but because I was the only girl, I never had to share a room. Why is this important? It means I had literally almost two decades to fine-tune my organizational process without being bothered or impeded by a roommate. But it wasn't just my room that was neat and tidy (and really, it wasn't so much neat and tidy as organized). It should be noted that one of my "selling qualities" to my husband was the fact that he perceived me to be a neat-freak. Later he realized I am more of an organization freak. How do those "freak" traits differ? Simple. One makes sure that all the books and compact discs are alphabetized and has an uncanny knack for the ability to recall what is in any drawer, closet, container, or cabinet in the house at any given time. (Although that trait doesn't seem to apply to keys and credit cards, which get misplaced daily.) The other is concerned with things like laundry, dirty dishes in the sink, and dust bunnies in the corner. This is not to say that I like living in filth (I can clean when need be), but there is a distinction between neat and organized. Now that we have made that distinction clearer and revealed my dirty little secrets, I would have to say that from about the age of four or five, I have reveled in my knack for organization whether it be archiving my own school papers (which I did from elementary through college) or generating my own to-do lists and taking inventory of my Beanie Babies and DVD collection. And unlike Beanie Babies and compact discs, organization wasn't a fad for me.

Fast-forward to my current job. Every year our team gets to vote for members of the group to be attributed with an adjective (kind of like a high school yearbook). Without fail, my senior superlative is "Most Organized." That's because, while everyone is reading or watching their favorite cinematic delicacies on a flight, I am . . . wait for it . . . organizing, renaming, and weeding/pruning my docs and folders on my laptop. If you are of my generation (the Xennials, balancing precariously on the precipice of Generation X and the Millennials) or simply had eighty-five hours to binge watch all two hundred thirty-eight episodes of the ten-season run of *Friends*, you might see me as Monica without the manic cleaning. Remember that episode where Chandler randomly put away the CDs in different CD cases based on the ones he listened to last. Seriously, that would drive me insane. If I were Monica and you were Chandler, we would pull an all-nighter to ensure that collection was free of orphan or mismatched CDs and that every case was in its proper place. To this day, I still organize my DVDs by genre (e.g., romance, blockbuster, classic, and compilation) and then alphabetically within that genre. And just like that time Monica took her label maker to Phoebe's apartment to help with packing so Mike (played by Paul Rudd) could move in, I too get a dopamine kick from reorganizing a room or even a cabinet. I haven't gone as far as inventorying my coffee mugs with a number to ensure that none go missing . . . so there's that.

Clearly, organization is part of who I am. It's in my bones and psyche, and seeing things lined up neatly on the shelf or in little color-coded folders on my screen just makes me happy. But the reason organization is so important to me is that it helps me find and do what I set out to find and do. I accomplish more when my mind, life, and surroundings are well organized than when things are scattered or in disarray. Which brings me to the next point . . .

1.2 Why Organization Is Important for Your Students

You have heard my story and know my sordid past but may not be moved to why organization is so important for us today as well as why it is so important for our students. I could wax intellectual about how there are actual stores (e.g., the Container Store) devoted to organization, times of year (e.g., spring cleaning) dedicated to it, and a bestselling book with more than twelve thousand Amazon reviews illuminating the art of it (e.g., *The Life-Changing Magic of Tidying Up: The Japanese Art of Decluttering and Organizing*). I could tell you that while content is taught with fidelity within the classrooms I see, study skills, organization, and note-taking skills are just a few soft skills that I have discovered are only taught in classes like MAPS (Methodology for Academic and Personal Success) or AVID (Advancement Via Individual Determination).

But what moves me to action is looking at colleges and careers and *providing students with skills that are transferable to whatever they choose to do after their time with us*. While writing my first book on the topic of communication, I found that these soft skills (social emotional learning skills) tended to top the charts for what employers were looking for in applicants. If you are familiar with CASEL's Social and Emotional Learning skills, this will sound familiar. If you aren't, I highly recommend visiting their site and checking out the five competencies: self-awareness, self-management, social awareness, relationship skills, and responsible decision-making. The first two chapters of this book focus on self-management, which breaks down into skills that fall under the umbrella of organization and time management. To truly understand why organization is so important, we must recognize the shift that has happened in the world and how it impacts our own thinking as well as how we approach the topic of organization with our students.

The first shift was away from the reliance on analog objects that held limited space for documents to digital objects that hold unlimited space. Think back to high school, college, or even your first year of teaching. I personally relied on a computer with a blinking orange cursor that took five-and-a-quarter-inch floppy discs in high school. That was replaced by my first Dell desktop (with a three-and-a-half-inch disc drive) in college. It wasn't till my first year of teaching that I discovered there was a better way to transfer documents from home to work than to burn them to a compact disc. I will never forget that day. My fellow teammate walked in wielding this magic object around his neck. It was a shiny, small USB drive (which, ironically, most of our current students have never seen or have only heard of). The fact that I could now take larger docs back and forth from home to school and not have to burn CDs was life changing. At that time, sharing documents was hocus pocus. I still had a filing cabinet brimming with handouts and a bookshelf with binders of transparencies, master copies, and pretty much everything I would need to dazzle seventh-grade students with fractions and decimals and percentages . . . *Oh, Pi!*

By all accounts, paperless classrooms and unlimited storage seemed like a step forward—a good thing. And with one exception, it was. I was easily able to manage all those files and housed them in two drawers of a four-drawer cabinet. A traditional four-drawer cabinet holds roughly 8,448 folders *or* approximately 2,500 pages per drawer. So at most, I imagine I had 5,000 pages, but to be fair, most of those were multiple copies of the same handout or test. By my last count on my personal computer, I have 29,573 individual files (most are multiple pages or multi-slide decks). That is six times what I had in my classroom. And if you do the math, most of those files in the cabinet were sets of twenty or thirty, which means I probably had at most two hundred individual files. Before we find ourselves full throttle in a Dan Meyer math video, I am narrowing in on a point: When files were limited to size or how many would fit in a filing cabinet (or on a disc), they were easier to manage. I could efficiently and tangibly take the wayward documents lying on my desk or on top of the filing cabinet and refile them with ease.

Yes, the ways of digital unlimited file abundance come standard with a search, but you must remember where you put the file—and there is typically more than one place to look. While I have nearly 30,000 individual files on my MacBook, I have another 1,400 in Evernote, 516 in my personal Google Drive account (not counting the 134 shared with me), and don't even get me started on my school Google Drive account (where many staff members by default share all their documents with all members of the organization). Oh, and let's not forget the 27,871 photos I have floating in cyberspace. So searching takes time.

File sharing and archiving isn't just limited to file services like Google Drive and Evernote. Files and websites are constantly shared via tools like Facebook, Twitter, Pinterest, Slack, Trello, email, text, and notes. And although search tools are getting better, they are still only as good as your memory. If you don't remember the service you used and/or a pretty good approximation of the name of the file (e.g., was it "Ed Tech Agenda," "ET Agenda," or "ET Meetings"?), then that file may as well be at the bottom of a well with no bucket to retrieve it. I am not ashamed to admit I have been in more than one meeting where I and/or another person in that meeting could not locate the shared agenda or spent the first ten to fifteen minutes of the meeting trying to find a slide deck or pertinent file. Sure, there are hacks like starring and favoriting files, but let's be honest, in the next five to ten years, it isn't like we are going to go back to the analog ages of the file cabinet. We are, in fact, going to continue to generate and store multitudes of documents and files, and I imagine we will want them to be easily accessible.

If adults experience the disappearing or hide-and-seek doc phenomenon, you can't very well expect our students to wield the magic locator ring the second they walk into your classroom. In this day and age, students don't just have tangible notes and binders. They have digital ones as well. While they may have learned the ins and outs of setting up a swank binder with colored tabs and a few sheet protectors in elementary or perhaps middle school, many of them have no idea where to begin when it comes to making sense of their digital files.

As an EdTech for a 1:1 iPad high school, my job is to provide PD and support to both staff and students alike. When we rolled out new devices, we spent a fair amount of time setting up accounts and familiarizing students with the iOS. While students tend to manage well enough with the devices today, one of the biggest issues I encounter is their ability to transfer the analog organization skills of the Trapper Keeper era to today. Yes, some are Type-A students who manage to neatly sort and store their digital resources. The vast majority, however, are waiting for a life raft. If I had a shilling for each time a student lost or misplaced a file, well, I would be living in a different country and century, but you get the idea.

When learners come into my office in a panic that they have lost a file or multiple files, it is typically due to one of two things:

- **Lack of understanding of how and where files are located—** They assume they can work at home under one Google account, and that document will be available under the school account because it is still "Google."

- **Lack of understanding of how and where files are saved—** Some users assume that, because it is digital, all files autosave;

likewise, people assume if they have an iCloud account on the device, Pages and Keynote will automatically back up files—forgetting about things like storage space or signing into the app.

If you erased a chalkboard or slate, you wouldn't expect the same writing to magically reappear the next day, but that is the equivalent of the unreasonable expectations created by some of the misunderstandings people have regarding file backups and retrieval. I realize this topic will continue to be quite fluid as cloud technology improves, Siri and Alexa become official personal assistants, and we provide a more streamlined approach for student work, but in the interim, I'll share some strategies for building a foundation of organizational structure and mindset throughout the rest of this chapter.

Many times I am able to retrieve files based on user error and provide some more information about file location and saving. But there is also that time when I can't. (It feels like an episode of *ER* or *Grey's Anatomy* in which they lose a patient. Well, not quite that dramatic, but almost!) It seriously breaks my heart sending away students who have lost an entire semester's worth of notes or all their college essays with no more than sincere condolences and a plan for not having it happen in the future. (This actually happened. A student had an issue with an app and lost all her college essays. Fortunately, she had emailed drafts of these to a teacher and a friend; otherwise, there would have been far more tears.) Like I said, as technology is rapidly changing, and many of you have countless scenarios that involve devices ranging from Chromebooks and shared carts to an iPad 1:1 or a cart of MacBooks, there is no point in providing you with an exhaustive list of all the possibilities and pathways for organization and archival. What I have learned over the past eight years as an EdTech supporting campuses with carts of iPods and iPads is that problems may change and evolve each year, but the answers don't.

1.3 Teach Your Students Basic Organization Skills That Will Last Them a Lifetime

I am a firm believer that the best way to raise organized students is to provide some scaffolding and guidance . . . which will ultimately ensure adoption and eventually autonomy and automaticity. For secondary students, I suggest a three-part plan. Before you review these strategies and processes, I should mention that, while you may not be using Notability or Google Classroom or Calendar with your students, the overarching topics and skills of organization, color coding, and having a backup can be applied to a variety of apps and tools, both analog and digital. Truthfully, most online note-taking tools boast similar functionality.

1.3a Provide a Portfolio with an Index

Provide a Portfolio. As more student work becomes digital in nature (or at the very least can be easily digitally archived), providing students with a scaffolded approach to organization is vital. Portfolios typically need to meet multiple needs. First and foremost, all students, teachers, and district personnel need to have access and familiarity with student portfolios. Google Classroom came along and met that need. When the online classroom platform rolled out, most people were already familiar enough with Google's tools that it wove seamlessly into the digital practices our teachers had already adopted. But if it were that easy, I certainly wouldn't be writing a chapter on organization.

When our school began using Google Classroom, the sharing of folders and access as well as organization was still confusing to say the least. How could students easily locate shared classroom docs after courses were archived or deleted? How did they organize their own work each year? The easiest answer included creating a Google Drive folder for each student that was pushed out manually via an add-on called Doctopus by the Technology Services department. Using that add-on streamlined and simplified the process so every student had a portfolio (or at the very least a glorified online system of shared folders) that every teacher could access from year to year and that students could use throughout their high school career.

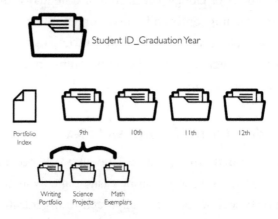

Figure 1.1: Sample folder structure for student portfolio using icons from Noun Project

Provide an Index. Within the folder structure (Figure 1.1), we included a portfolio index template (Figure 1.2). This document was nothing more than a glorified Google Doc with tables, bullets, and prompts, but the intent was to have it serve as a thoughtful table of contents within the portfolio folder. Ultimately we wanted the portfolio to be less of a dumping ground for documents and more of a way to curate work for later access and review.

Name: Graduation Year: 2019

MY GOALS for ME as a LEARNER:	
ONGOING REFLECTIONS: *(Consider using prompts from Austin Kleon or Leonardo da Vinci to support this)* *Austin Kleon:* • 10 Things I Could've Done But Didn't • 10 Things I Want to Learn • 10 Questions I Have • 10 Things That Are Going Great Right Now • Thanks to _____ who Taught me _____ . • What Excites You? / What Drains You? *Leonardo da Vinci:* • Who are my most inspiring role models? • List 3 of your strengths and weaknesses. How are these related? • What people, places, and activities allow me to feel most fully myself? • What is my ideal working environment? • Think of an important goal you accomplished. Note the process you utilized to accomplish it.	

MY LEARNING ARTIFACTS and EXEMPLARS:	
PROJECT EXEMPLAR:	• LINK HERE • LINK HERE • LINK HERE
WRITING EXEMPLAR(S):	• LINK HERE • LINK HERE • LINK HERE

PROBLEM-SOLVING EXEMPLAR:	• LINK HERE • LINK HERE • LINK HERE

ADDITIONAL LEARNING ARTIFACTS and EXEMPLARS:	
BLOG:	• LINK HERE
PORTFOLIO:	• LINK HERE
AWARDS, HONORS, COMMITTEES, CLUBS, VOLUNTEER:	• AWARD • HONOR • ACCOLADE • COMMITTEES • CLUBS • VOLUNTEER

Figure 1.2: Portfolio Index created with Google Docs featuring prompts from Austin Kleon[1] and Michael Gelb[2]

Before we get too far into the File-O-Dex Forest, I should mention that we use what we call "base camp" training (Figure 1.3) to deploy these portfolios and organizational strategies. Students come to our high school from different campuses and/or transfer in from other districts, which can make it difficult to ensure a level playing field when it comes to the basics. For us, the basics revolve around tools and processes that students need in place to be successful in their classes. The base camp model is designed to provide students with a baseline of skills early in the school year. With that in mind, we devote a whole day to ensuring our entire freshman class has these skills (e.g., access to a portfolio, ability to navigate and organize their notes within Notability, access to all of their classes in Google Calendar, and one other station that we modify from year to year

Figure 1.3: Students and iPad Base Camp

based on campus needs). Resources to support the ideas in this book as well as more on this topic of base camps can be found on my site techchef4u.com/books including a link to all the stations and a slide deck explaining the process and logistics.

1.3b Teach Them a Plan They Can Apply to Other Apps

It's one thing to teach learners how to use a portfolio and organizational system for a single platform, but we can't stop there. The next step is to teach them a step-by-step plan and/or organizational structure they can apply to any app. While the following plan is delineated using the Notability app (which we regularly use K–12), I encourage you to adopt a similar structure for organization in any apps in which students regularly create content and take notes. During our base camp time, we set up a Notability station where students learn to complete four tasks:

1. **Archive old stuff.** We instructed students to create an "Old Stuff" or "Eighth Grade" folder, not because we want them to be professional digital hoarders but so old docs weren't cluttering or distracting their current notebooks. (This is a shift from when we burned old notebooks from year to year. Who I am kidding? I kept all my dialectical notebooks, but I did know a handful of students who relished a proper fire ceremony at the end of each year.) If they wanted to access old documents, notes, or papers, they still could, but their Notability was nice and tidy for the upcoming year.

2. **Take and manage digital notes.** In apps like Notability and even OneNote, we explained the difference between a divider and a folder and shared in what instances one would use one system over the other. Students thought about their classes and decided which classes lent themselves to subcategories (e.g.,

in Spanish, you might have separate categories for vocabulary and assignments or organize it by unit) and which didn't (e.g., in math, you might decide to keep all assignments together in one folder called Math rather than creating subfolders for each chapter or topic).

3. **Color-Code course folders.** In this digital and sharing age, it is so easy and ephemeral to create a new doc or folder. In the analog age, each class might claim a certain color folder or notebook, and students knew to organize that way. That practice persists at the elementary level. To simplify the process of randomly colored class calendars and folders, we decided on colors for departments (grades six through twelve). This way every time a student had a social studies class, they would color-code calendars and folders red, and every time they had a science class, they would use green. Once we devised this format, students had a consistent nomenclature to use when organizing their folders that they could apply across a variety of apps and tools.

4. **Back up their Google Drive.** The most important piece was having them turn on automatic Google Drive Backup. Because Notability is one of those apps that doesn't have an automatic account tied to it (like Google, Thinglink, Haiku Deck, etc.), we wanted to ensure that no note was ever lost. I would call this the Digital Shepherd approach. I would highly advise that students know how, where, and if their content is being stored and backed up.

If we are going to pull students out of classes for our Base Camp, I want that time to be well spent and for students to gain something from it. To be certain, I employ the practice of exit tickets. For the

Base Camp, I typically only ask one question: "What was the most impactful thing you learned and/or will use from today?"

Interestingly, more than 25 percent of the students I polled at our last few Base Camps responded, "Notability." Many of their responses praised the ability to be organized, make folders, change colors, and properly use the app. And if that wasn't enough, several students noted that the instructions and guides they received during Base Camp were helpful. They expressed appreciation for the time they were given to set up apps, become familiar with new features, and ultimately get organized. I also want to note that I realize every campus doesn't always have an EdTech on staff who is responsible for planning and putting on a Base Camp, but this model can be adapted easily to stations at the beginning of school or modified to have each core content area take a station and deliver that in their class. The content could also be recreated in videos or in an iTunes U or Google Classroom course. It is less about the delivery and more about the consistent structures employed within the stations. Equally important is the time to allow students to get organized and familiarize themselves with the apps and tools they will be using all year long.

1.3c Get Them Thinking about Devising and Adopting a Plan for Notes

About six to eight weeks after our Freshman iPad Base Camp, our academic interventionist asked if I would like to help do a session on study skills and note-taking. As I love doing PD with students, I jumped at the opportunity. To get a better feel for what a student experienced in school, I sent out a survey to the staff that asked a variety of questions about note-taking (which will be revealed in Chapter 3) and organization. From multiple student encounters and observations, I have also learned that the majority of students (and if

I am being totally honest, adults too) do not have a digital organization system in place. While I couldn't possibly plan for every app and type of file students will encounter in the rest of their academic lives and in their careers, I knew that I could get them thinking about this topic. Focused on the intention of empowering learners to devise and adopt their own plan for digital organization, I used the session to remind them of the skills they learned at the Notability station at the Freshman iPad Base Camp and then shared with them my system for organization (Figure 1.4). I made it very clear that my process is not a one-size-fits-all system—and that our systems change with the seasons of our lives. What I wanted them to understand is that what I shared was simply my process. My goal was to get them thinking about developing their own strategies for organization. After all, if they devised an effective plan and put it into action before college or their career, they would be in a far better place than most adults are now.

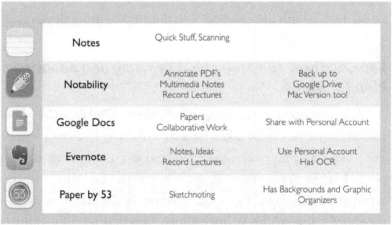

Figure 1.4: My Organizational Plan

The process that I shared was fairly simple. It only applies to digital work and really had student workflow in mind:

- **Notes:** I only use notes for quick stuff like a store list, something I need to write down quickly, and to scan something.

- **Notability:** I would use this to annotate PDFs and handouts, create multimedia notes, and record lectures.

- **Google Docs:** This would be for writing papers and doing collaborative work, as it has so many add-ons and is such a robust word-processing tool.

- **Evernote:** I personally would use this for notes, ideas, and to record lectures that you plan on typing. Unlike Notability it is available on every device, and you can tag notes with keywords, which makes this perfect to use from year to year.

- **Paper by 53:** This is for sketchnoting or visual note-taking, as it boasts multiple drawing tools.

I'll share a slightly different process in Chapter 3 for my analog notes. I also only mentioned apps and processes that applied exclusively to schoolwork and the academic setting. I would have added a few more had I been talking about organizing both my personal (TechChef4u) and professional (EdTech) resources.

1.3d Suggest a Central Location for Everything Else

We as educators serve as role models, leaders, and guides for our students. While the majority of this chapter is devoted to what we can do for students, I think it is also vital to address the processes and digital pathways we devise to share content online for our students and with other educators around the world. Ideally, we don't want to create and curate content for our students that disappears from year to year or that is not easily found. We also want to model best practices for how we create and curate online and vet new tools.

Recently I did an audit (Figure 1.5) of all the sites to which I had published content. I had five Smores, five bulbs, five Haiku Decks, six Scoopit categories, twelve Snapguides, thirteen Slideshare uploads (encompassing decks and infographics), nineteen Quizlets, eighty-three Listlys, and ninety-one Thinglinks.

Figure 1.5: Tool/Site/Service Audit featuring IKEA sea life stickers and Dylusions stickers by Dyan Reaveley

The list might sound like a wizardry school supply list for Hogwart's, but it is more like a spiderweb of an online professional portfolio. My modern apothecary online shop formula equates to this (Figure 1.6): I use Smores to curate large topics for PD. I use bulbs to create differentiated PD, as its design allows users to create a collection and multiple pages within a collection. I use Thinglinks to strategically place links and resources on an image. I use Snapguides to illustrate a step-by-step process, and I use Listlys to curate collections of apps.

Pinterest	Pinterest	Use to organize and archive ideas, research, lessons, etc...
Thinglink	Thinglink	Use to create webquests, interactive infographics, and interactive notes.
L	list.ly	Use to create lists of resources, sites, or apps to be viewed in a linear fashion.
S	Snapguide	Use to create multimedia guides and tutorials.
Q	Quizlet	Use to create sorting games of SAMR vocabulary for professional development OR to create tasks for stations that can be done in any order.

Figure 1.6: Table of apps and purpose of each

Whether you use these tools or you prefer a Prezi in a pear tree, I hope this list gets you thinking:

- **Take Inventory of the Sites:** How many sites have you and/or your students accounts for? On how many do you publish content?

- **Evaluate the Purpose of the Site:** What is the unique purpose of each site/app/tool?

- **Weed Dated or Old Sites/Content:** Are there any sites/tools you no longer use? Or are there resources and content that need to be updated or removed?

- **Devise a Central Repository:** Do you have a central site or portfolio for your students or yourself to link all your content published on third-party sites?

The first two bullets assist with taking stock of and evaluating the content and tools that you have and/or utilize. The last helps you and your students locate content in an organized fashion. For me and our students, a central repository was not even a thing until recently. I fixed my own problem by creating a portfolio site on my blog for my work (Figure 1.7), and our student problem was fixed by utilizing the portfolio index mentioned earlier in the chapter.

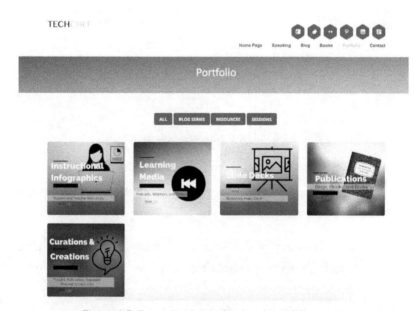

Figure 1.7: Example of a professional portfolio using Wordpress techchef4u.com/portfolio

As I mentioned, I use a variety of services to share and archive digital media, ranging from texts and tweets to blogs and pins. When Tackk (a service like Smore that allows people to create multimedia web scrolls) closed its doors in September of 2017, I immediately grabbed my eleven Tackks and downloaded them as PDFs. These were multimedia documents that I had created to collect info on topics (e.g., ePortfolios, SAMR, Tools for 1:1 or BYOD) and had made public so other people could benefit from them. (Before the site was taken down, my "Tools for 1:1" document had 39,000 visits, and my Tackk on ePortfolios had 137,000). I didn't realize how many people were using my document until a teacher in Maine emailed me to ask if I had the ePortfolio Tackk, because she and her students used it every year, and the link had suddenly died. Fortunately I had downloaded the PDF version, which I quickly emailed to her.

I delve into this story to serve as a greater reminder that in this sharing economy, in addition to being intentional about organizing digital content for ourselves, we might also want to be more prudent as we select services and create and organize content that will be available to others. Nobody cares what is on my desktop or in my personal drives, but when we start sharing documents with others (with students, colleagues, or the greater "edusphere"), be it through Google Drive or Smore, Haiku Deck, or Thinglink, people start relying on that front-facing content. Whether or not you use these apps and tools, I hope the bigger takeaway is devising your own plan for perennial content curation and creation as well as a central repository.

1.3e Devise Strategies for Vetting Digital Tools/Apps

Now before you get your magic locator ring for centralizing and streamlining digital content, I want to throw out one more suggestion: As you devise your personal plan for digital organization, create a list of questions to help you (and your learners) evaluate new tools and sites. I've shared my criteria below, but before you read my list, I should mention that I am all for being a File Floozie; there is no risk with trying a new site or tool. It is nothing like buying shoes that, once you break them in or take them for a walk, you can't very well return. When it comes to tools and apps, try as many as you like, and only commit to the ones that meet your criteria. The criteria I require all tools and apps to meet are listed below. You and your school or district might have different criteria in mind, so this list of considerations and demands below may vary for you.

- **Is it in beta?** Beta is not a bad thing. There are many sites that have started out in beta and become staples of our classroom. The thing to remember about apps or platforms in beta is not to put all your eggs in one beta basket.

- **Do I want to share or just have private?** Tools and apps can serve multiple purposes. I use Evernote because it is simple and easy to organize. While it does have sharing capabilities, I don't typically use them. Sharing also implies collaboration. Thinglink and Canva both have sharing capabilities, but they don't really support real-time collaboration the way a Google Doc does.

- **What type of formatting options do I need, and which ones does it offer?** Before I choose a new tool, I look at what it offers; for example, while I like Adobe Spark Post, it is so similar to Canva to me in its formatting and features that I don't need to use both. An extension to this question might be "What type of multimedia can I include?" One site may allow embedding tools, and another might only allow uploading of files.

- **How do I export my content if need be?** As I mentioned with Tackk (and could rant on about at least two or three other sites that shut down leaving my content in the land of Digital Purgatory), the ability to export content is important, especially for our students. If they use a portfolio tool, they should be able to easily remove and carry away that content when they graduate or leave the district.

I used to be a bit of an EdTech Kramer. I would bounce into a classroom and say, "Hey, have you heard about Thinglink? Let me tell you about Nearpod. OMG, do know how Haiku Deck will revolutionize how your students deliver presentations?" While I was and am still enamored with these sites, they are not always the right fit for everyone.

When we were looking at a new portfolio system for our school, I got to thinking about the last few jumps we had made, and it made me feel a little bit like we had been island hopping. Each time we find a new tool, a few people swim over to the next island and figure it out. When they have it figured out, they send word, and most of the inhabitants swim on over to the next island. But we always leave people behind. And sometimes the new island isn't even stable; in fact, sometimes the new island sinks or implodes, as was the case with Tackk. I am certainly not saying that we need to be the last to embrace change or that we shouldn't scout out new lands and visit innovative products, I am just saying that in an economy that thrives on endless choices and is constantly plagued by decision paralysis, sometimes it is important to make sure that you are making the best choice for all parties involved. We must ask ourselves, "Do I need to swim to the next island?" In other words, *Do I really need another new app?*

1.4 Creatively Organize Your Desktop to Maximize Productivity

Most of this chapter has focused on web tools and apps. All of these are important, but you most likely also work on laptops and/or desktops, or you may even have a 1:1 laptop situation for your students. Several years ago, I was introduced to the idea of custom desktop wallpapers. Essentially, you create a graphic organizer for your files on your desktop. I like to change mine every year just for fun. I am one of those people who tidies her desk before leaving my office every day, and my computer desktop gets the same treatment. If unfiled files and screenshots are cluttering my screen, I find it distracting and difficult to locate what I need. If you like to play with graphics, you can spend quite a bit of time creating your desktop organizer, or you can save a ton of time and download one; they are plentiful on Pinterest. Whenever people see my desktop (Figure 1.8a), they inevitably comment they would like one of their own, so each

Figure 1.8a: Personal Example of Desktop Organizer created with Unsplash, Fuzzimo, and Keynote. Unsplash photo by LUM3N

year I create one for my staff that has the bell schedule or one that is designed for a specific content area (Figure 1.8b).

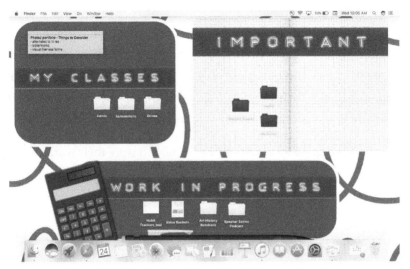

Figure 1.8b: Professional Example of Desktop Organizer
created with Fuzzimo and Canva

I hope the biggest takeaway for you with this chapter is that organization is the need to take a mindful approach to our work and our creations. Organization, like any skill, takes practice. And like buying shoes, you need to try on a few things that fit before finding the ones that are just right. No one has time to organize the digital chaos left in the wake of a tenure of teaching, but hopefully this chapter provides some ideas to start supporting the structure and process of organization in the classroom and in life. It has taken me many years to really hone a system that works for me (both analog and digital). Organization (unlike calculus, #sorrynotsorry) is one of those skills that if taught with fidelity can be transferable to other realms of our lives, including how we manage our days, how we set goals, how we take notes, and how we organize in IRL (in real life). All of which we will delve into as we move further down the rabbit hole.

AWESOME AMULET CHECKLIST

I find that after I read a chapter (even if I highlight as I go or take notes in the margin), a quick checklist is helpful to summarize the material and to revisit when I want to review or act on the information. While I am certainly not trying to standardize the content shared, I do like writing these as learning targets because I think it makes it easier for people to figure out which ones they and their learners have mastered and which ones are still a work in progress.

☐ My students have a digital portfolio to store their work.

☐ My students have an index and/or a table of contents for their portfolio.

☐ My students understand file structure and systems.

☐ My students can back up and share their digital work across multiple accounts and interfaces (e.g., Google Drive, Notability, third-party apps, etc.).

☐ My students can do basic troubleshooting to recover a file (e.g., search their browser history, double-check which account they were in, etc.).

☐ My students have a plan and structure for organizing their digital notes.

☐ My students can archive old schoolwork from year to year.

☐ My students have a personal process for taking and storing a variety of different media (e.g., notes in Evernote, sketches in Paper by 53, papers in Google Docs).

☐ My students can evaluate and choose the best tool for the job based on criteria like collaboration, formatting, and file sharing.

These statements could also be used as qualifiers for the folder organization badge (or amulet) too.

WAKEFUL WHIMSY CORE IDEAS

I tried to provide a device and content-neutral space for you to explore and frolic. I know many people like curricular ideas, and a few can be very potent. So without further ado, I wanted to share some whimsical ways you could integrate these ideas into core curriculum. These are certainly not meant to be comprehensive but simply provide a springboard for additional opportunities:

- **English Language Arts:** Have students create an online portfolio index for an author or literary character. What exemplars would they include? What awards and honors have they received? How would they use the tools we have today? What tools would Poe use religiously? Would Emily Dickinson post all her poems to Haiku Deck?

- **Math:** Have students create a flowchart or mind map for how they organize their documents or digital work or a decision tree for choosing new tools.

- **Science:** Have students research the scientific and/or health benefits of being organized.

- **Social Studies:** Have students create a desktop organizer or a folder structure for a historical figure. What would the titles of their folders be? Would they be messy or meticulous? Do some research on color psychology and determine which colors the figure would use to color-code with. Based on what you know of the historical figure, their personality, and their contributions, what would be some of the names of their files and folders?

SHARE YOUR OWN EXAMPLES AND IDEAS INSPIRED BY THIS CHAPTER. BE SURE TO TAG YOUR COMMENTS: #CREATIVELYPRODUCTIVE.

Citations

1. Kleon, Austin. *The Steal like an Artist Journal.* New York, New York: Workman Publishing Company, 2015.

2. Gelb, Michael. *How to Think like Leonardo Da Vinci.* New York, New York: Bantam Dell, 2004.

Research

- CASEL. 2018. "Core SEL Competencies." *Casel.org.* casel.org/core-competencies

- ILM Corporation. "Estimate the Number of Pages or Images—ILM Corporation." *ILM Corporation.* ilmcorp.com/tools-and-resources/estimate-the-number-of-pages-or-images.

- Smead. "Shelf Filing Vs. Drawer Filing: Which is Best For Your Office?" *Smead.* smead.com/Director.aspx?NodeId=1628.

Chapter 2

Taming Time

Oh dear! Oh dear! I shall be too late!

—Rabbit, Alice's Adventures in Wonderland

Amulet: Calendar

When I think of time and calendars, the white rabbit hippity hops into my brain. Unfortunately he tends to be chronically late, so perhaps he is not the best example of time management now that I think about it. With technology that allows us to do more, connect 24/7, and create almost anything from a mobile device or a laptop, we wear busy as a badge. As technologies evolve and improve, I don't think our lives are magically going to get any less busy. You may have fond memories of a simpler time—a time of dial-up modems, typewriters, sixteen-bit video games, Kodak film, and dot matrix printers. But for our students, the simpler time is now. Life, for them or for us, is never going to be simpler as far as technology and constant connection are concerned. That means this is the time to teach them the best way to navigate "busy." After all, there is no way to create more hours in the day or week (unless you gain some vampiric qualities of not needing to sleep, at which point you may also gain the ability to shimmer in the sun, so there's that). Even though we cannot create more time, there are ways to make the most out of those 168 hours we are given each week. Making the best use of the time we have is essential as we become responsible for more at work and at home, and that need is magnified by the fact that so much of that for which we are responsible is digital (e.g., emails, slide decks, websites), and we can't touch it. It isn't like walking past a stack of papers and knowing they need to be graded or standing in front of a room of parents with their hands raised. Those parents now send communications that pile up in our email or stack up in our voice-mail, and those papers waiting to be assigned a grade are often digital. How we choose to navigate this new digital world and what we do to not only be efficient and productive but to make the most of our time in class, at work, and in life, can mean all the difference between the constant worry of "I'm late, I'm late!" and living with a sense of peace and accomplishment.

2.1 Why Calendars, Planners, and Bullet Journals Are Important Today

Most organized people rely on a calendar and a to-do list. I feel lost at sea without mine. Leaving my to-do list at home is the equivalent of forgetting my phone, and I have returned home for it . . . and my mason jar of assorted, colored Sharpie fine-tip pens. I have interviewed people in a variety of industries ranging from nursing and architecture to business, social media, and makeup and hair artistry, and I have discovered a simple trend: The majority used a digital calendar for appointments and meetings. But when it comes to to-do lists, the data tells a different story. In this case, 35 percent of participants used a digital to-do list and 48 percent used a blend of both digital and analog. In the case of calendars and to-do lists, it is less important what tool you use, and more important that it works for you. Not using them—or forgetting to put an important item on a to-do list or calendar—leads to missed meetings, appointments, birthdays, and deadlines. In some cases, these lapses in memory and time management have cost people their job or given them a reputation of being less than dependable. If we aim to prepare our learners to succeed in school and thrive beyond our walls, they need to know how to manage their time well.

Perhaps a jaunt to Office Depot doesn't fill you with glee. Perhaps you don't scope out end caps for clearance office supplies. I know some people think calendars and to-do lists are super boring or like eating cauliflower or something. Not me. The intriguing thing to me about calendars and to-do lists is that they really have evolved over time and become so personalized through the technologies of both digital calendars and the ability to design your own. The days of CD-Roms of desktop publishing and clipart have paved the way to today's personalized to-do lists and calendars. Entire Etsy shops are filled with time-taming printables. To give you an idea of how pervasive the planner DIY Etsy trend is, consider this: A search for "planner printables" and "planner stickers" will produce upwards of 103,000 and 320,000 results respectively.

As with many trends, oftentimes it starts out as a form of hobby or edutainment and then quickly gains merit for its educational and professional purpose. I am starting to see that happen with paper planners and bullet journaling. With articles like "11 Reasons You Should Ditch Your Smartphone for a Planner," "What Happened When I Ditched My Smartphone for a Paper Planner," and "Why Paper Is the Real 'Killer App,'" from well-respected entities like *BuzzFeed*, *Fast*

Company, and *BBC*, one has to wonder if shifting back to paper is a fad or something more permanent.

If I were a betting lady, these following planner stats would at the very least make me take note of the trend. The same year that Steve Jobs released the generation 1 iPhone, Erin Condren released her Life Planner. In a time when everyone thought the iPhone would serve all the scheduling and calendar needs of a generation, two million people purchased a Life Planner. Fast-forward eight years to April 2015, The Happy Planner company launched their first planner and sold more than five million planners in three years. Over the years, Erin Condren has become a staple of the planner community, and in 2018 she opened up a storefront for her personalized planners right here in my hometown of Austin, Texas. Wild for Planners started an annual planner conference in 2016 which has sold out every year since its debut. I am not ashamed to admit that I attended the Austin Wild for Planners event in 2018, and I can tell you that it is hands down one of my favorite events.

I have always used to-do lists religiously, and planners were very much a part of my life in high school and in college. As calendars became digital, I tried to keep afloat and ride the wave but found that I was sinking. It wasn't until I got a Passion Planner three years ago and began a bullet journal around the same time that I realized many more educators and students were, like me, hungry for a process that worked.

If there were just a few people in far-off places taking to the planner and bullet journaling front, I may have been dissuaded from pursuing these endeavors. But every door I cracked led to another door more intricate and intriguing than the next. And this is how I knew I was onto something. There are global Bullet Journaling Facebook groups. Two of them I joined have more than thirteen thousand combined members. I even discovered a group called "Journaling on the

Job: ProJos" that has almost fourteen thousand members. I also found the Planners Gone Wild Facebook group that has an online community of over sixty thousand members. So clearly there is at least an interest in this art form and process in the professional realm as well.

Now before I get too far down the rabbit hole with planners and bullet journals, I feel I ought to distinguish between the two. Planners are typically a structured notebook that includes a printed weekly and monthly view and some places for reflections or a to-do list. Bullet Journals are used in a very similar fashion as a planner and offer very similar features but are typically blank and therefore far more customizable to the learner's needs. If one were to ask what a bullet journal is, please know that it is far more than a journal with bulleted lists.

The term and worldwide phenomenon, bullet journaling, is somewhat misleading, as it really is more of a planner on steroids than a traditional journal. It's really the convergence of a to-do list, planner, and diary. As my bullet journal has evolved over the past few years, it has become more than just a planner and a journal; it's a scrapbook and a writer/reader's notebook (Figure 2.1). Ryder Carroll, a New York designer, is credited with the creation of the official bullet journal, and the internet hasn't looked back since. Trusted news sites including *The Wall Street Journal* and *Los Angeles Times* have covered the topic. Lifestyle sites, such as Martha Stewart and Marie Claire, have as well. Even the well-known business-focused Bloomberg site posted the article "Bullet Journaling: Your Solution for Daily Disorganization;" thus, calendars, planners, to-do lists, and bullet journaling seem like not only the next fitting course to build on chapter one but essentials to prepare our students for the life and work outside of our institution. My intent isn't just to share these trends and practices but to highlight them and expose you to how they can be adapted to impact the lives of your students and your own personal and professional lives.

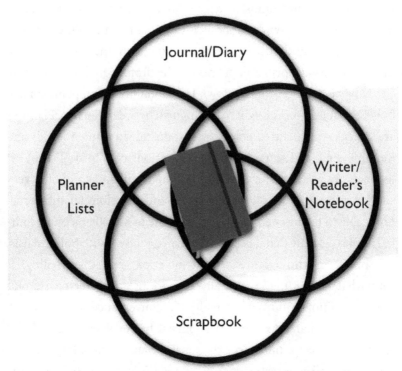

Figure 2.1: Venn Diagrams of what a bullet journal is and/or can be.

2.2 How to Teach Students the Basics of Using a Calendar, Planner, or Bullet Journal

There are countless options when it comes to calendars, planners, and bullet journals. Some are analog, and some are digital; some change with the seasons of our lives, and none of them are really one-size-fits-all. This is why I try to take the labor out of the labyrinth and provide multiple practical pathways. As with any organizational tool or system, the real key to success is exploration and error.

2.2a Digital Calendar Basics

Most teachers provide some sort of classroom calendar, be it a Google Calendar, a PDF, or a daily or weekly agenda written on the classroom whiteboard. As more schools adopt online classrooms environments (e.g., Edmodo, Schoology, Google Classroom, Canvas, etc.), many also offer calendars in a digital format. One benefit to online calendars is that you can access them from your digital devices—wherever you are. The downside to all calendars being digital is two-fold: The first is that digital calendars are like hitting the easy button that takes the ownership and responsibility off the student. For as much as there's a benefit to going digital, with technological progress, we must consider what skills may get left by the wayside—and what skills we need to intentionally cultivate in our students in light of the calendar express lane being added to the scholastic expressway. The second concern is the inherent distraction. When was the last time you spent forty-five minutes distracted by all the tabs in your planner while you were supposed to be checking your schedule for tomorrow? And just because our learners' (students *or* adults) calendars are threaded in one spot and sends them notifications doesn't mean they know how to manage time, set goals, and/or organize their tasks in an efficient way. Honestly, I think the beauty of analog, when it comes to calendars and to-do lists, is that it frees up distractions and forces you to slow down and really focus on what matters and how you are going to achieve it.

I use—and teach learners to use—digital calendars and analog planners in tandem. Most jobs don't have a neatly scheduled day of seven or eight time blocks; rather, they allow for large amounts of autonomy within the structure of the day. With such autonomy comes great responsibility to effectively analyze tasks, goals, and projects and schedule one's day accordingly. That reality means our students must learn to be fluent in the language of time management if they are going to succeed long term. Much of the end of this chapter will deal with autonomy and time management, so for digital calendars, I suggest a few actions to ensure fluency and productivity:

- **Access:** Make sure students have access to all their class calendars.

- **Color-Code:** Color-code calendars for easy access and viewing.

- **Weed:** Unsubscribe to old class calendars.

- **Take Control:** Learn how to set reminders and create events on the calendars rather than exclusively use them as passive reminders.

2.2b Planner Basics

Working at a 1:1 iPad high school with what we refer to as mobile natives, I expected most students to be all digital, as every teacher posts a Google Calendar for their class. When I co-taught a session on note-taking and digital organization, we came prepared with boxes of planners to hand out to students who were interested and assumed we would most likely pass out a handful. Two intriguing findings came out of that session: First, we discovered that almost half of our freshman students already had a planner for the school year. Second, when we offered to hand out planners to any student who asked for one, we got no takers. When we placed them on the tables that students were sitting around and told them they could take one if they needed it, lo and behold, not one planner crumb remained on the tables when the bell rang. The big realization for me was that freshman need planners, and while most of them will take action and get their own, a large portion of those who need a planner won't ask for one.

Many institutions purchase planners for their students or offer them in a school store. At some point, learners like to have the autonomy of purchasing their own. If you have students that want to do so, know that planners can be both analog and digital. If you or your students are looking for an analog one, there are many variations to take into consideration. Is it bound or a spiral? Does it come with accessories (e.g., add-ons or stickers)? Does it have a space for reflections? Does it include additional features like a ribbon bookmark or a back pocket? All of these are preferences to consider.

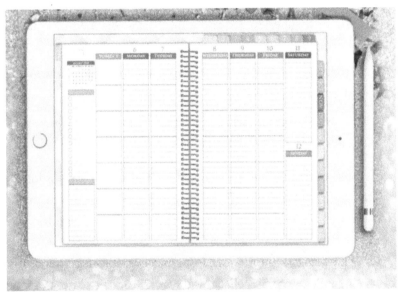

Figure 2.2: Student Planner for iPad created by @iPadPlanner on Instagram (PhotoMaterial.etsy.com)

And please know that you don't have to look to apps for digital planners. If you search Etsy for "digital planner," you will easily discover over forty thousand results. You can also look for "digital planner iPad pro" or "digital planner GoodNotes." Both @BohoBerry and @iPadPlanner (Figure 2.2) on Instagram have one they sell that works in conjunction with a PDF annotation app, so these are excellent alternatives for any learner who wants to have a planner but also wants to stay digital.

2.2c Bullet Journaling Basics

While I share both analog and digital options, calendars and planners are nothing new per se. On the other hand, bullet journals are and require a bit more discussion. Any time I mention bullet journals (aka "bujo"), learners respond in one of three ways:

1. They are super excited and want to show me their own bullet journals.

2. They have heard of bullet journals but don't know how to start their own.

3. They have no idea what a bullet journal is but are two-parts curious and one-part credulous.

Bullet journaling has been touted as "the analog system for the digital age"[1], as it is the perfect mix of organization, customization, and no-pressure journaling. The basic premise is that you draw out your week and then use a key to "bullet" your daily to-do list. Figure 2.3a depicts a high school student example, Figure 2.3b highlights the same student's journal in college, and Figure 2.3c showcases the most recent iteration of the that college student's journal which is actually the Hobonichi week planner. She mentioned that the methods prior to the Hobonichi were causing undue stress because things weren't getting done due to the fact that that particular journal/planner didn't provide the space to plan ahead. It is important to remember that our processes evolve with the seasons of our life so what may have worked in high school may not necessarily work when a student gets to college or enters the workforce.

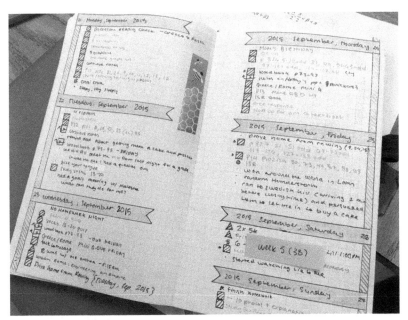

Figure 2.3a: High School Bullet journal weekly layout
by student Dana M.

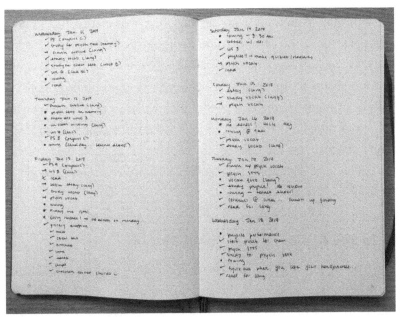

Figure 2.3b College Bullet journal weekly layout by student Dana M.

Figure 2.3c: College Bullet journal weekly layout
by student Dana M. using a Hobonichi week planner

For those who want to go full bujo, one must start with a key; for example, some people color-code their classes, and others use symbols. I've included a sample bullet journal from a Dutch UX designer, @dotted.plans on Instagram in Figure 2.4 as an example. The list of people to follow at the end of the book will also provide a treasure trove of examples if you want to follow the white rabbit. Even if you don't decide to go the bujo route, teaching students to devise a color-coded system or a key is truly beneficial for whatever calendar or to-do lists they end up using.

2.2d The Basics of a Personal System

Throughout this book, I try to share my process not because I want you to replicate it exactly (although you could) but because once someone sees a process, they can begin to analyze what might work

Figure 2.4: Example of bullet journal Key
created by Michenou (@dotted.plans on Instagram)

for them and what might not. I have a bit of a hybrid system (Figure 2.5) for calendars and time management:

- **Google Calendar:** I have both a personal and professional Google Calendar where I add all the events and appointments.

- **Paper Planner:** I also have a paper planner (actually a Passion Planner) where I write down big appointments and events and keep all my to-do lists. The Passion Planner forces me to really goal set my month rather than just add events on the fly; for example, the month view includes sections for People to See, Places to Go, Not-to-Do List, and Personal Projects and Work Projects lists. The Passion Planner also includes a section for monthly reflection, with six questions (which I mention in Chapter 5).

- **Bullet Journal:** I use my bullet journal for habit and mood tracking (more in Chapter 4), lists and reflections (Chapter 5), and writing about books I read (Chapter 6). I have also expanded its use to include some Productivity Bingo and Doodle a Day.

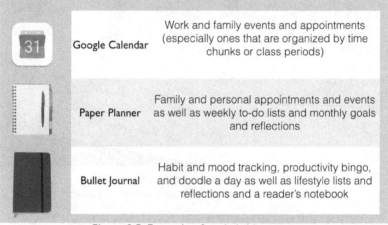

31	Google Calendar	Work and family events and appointments (especially ones that are organized by time chunks or class periods)
	Paper Planner	Family and personal appointments and events as well as weekly to-do lists and monthly goals and reflections
	Bullet Journal	Habit and mood tracking, productivity bingo, and doodle a day as well as lifestyle lists and reflections and a reader's notebook

Figure 2.5: Example of my hybrid process
of calendar, planner, and bullet journal

When I started meeting with students to talk about calendars and time management, it became clear to me that students fell into one of three categories: The first group of students included those who had some form of a planner and were using it but were open to ideas on how to use it better.

The second group comprised students who had a planner (most likely given to them or purchased by a parent) and literally had no idea what to do with it. Many times those planners weren't just a basic month-and week view but beefed-up, all-in-one planner/journals. For the student who is just trying to get by, these fancy, complicated planners can be highly overwhelming. I remember effusively praising one student on her use of her planner and her meticulous handwriting, only to have her tell me frankly that her mom filled it out for her because she was so overwhelmed by the tool. Telling students to use a planner isn't unlike telling children to clean their rooms. For some the task is straightforward. For others it seems complex and insurmountable; they have no idea how to break the large task into smaller pieces, such as hanging up your clean clothes in the closet, putting the dirty clothes in the hamper, making your bed, etc.

The third type of students is those who haven't even thought about a planner and have no idea that their classes are even in Google Calendar. Understanding the needs of these three very different groups of students led me to reevaluate the tools and the processes I was sharing with them. While I firmly believe students can handle a planner or a bullet journal, I also realized that most need to have the skill scaffolded and that they need easier points of entry. The rest of this chapter is designed to do just that by providing tips, strategies, and tools to teach learners to break down processes into a task and productively manage time.

2.3 How to Teach Students to Break Down a Process or Project

One of the biggest issues I see with students (and adults) related to time management is the inability to break down a task. The first step is helping students understand the difference between a task and a project. Tasks are typically something that can be completed in a day or a small span of time, whereas a project is something that could take far longer than a day and be made up of a series of smaller tasks. Writing a research paper would be an example of a project. Within the process of writing a research paper there would be smaller tasks like researching, revising, editing, etc. Too often students become overwhelmed by a project because they don't have the skills to break down the project into smaller pieces. People in a variety of careers experience both daily tasks and long-term projects. Below are four strategies that can be used to break down large ideas into smaller manageable tasks and eventually to-do lists.

2.3a Mind Mapping a Project or a Semester List

For planning projects, I use a mind map. I feel like the best way to combat task avoidance is to identify and illustrate all the pieces that need to be in place (or all the steps) to complete a project. Figure 2.6 is a mind map I crafted in the last stages of editing for the book you are now reading. If I just wrote "edit the book" on a list, this would be an overwhelming task. I prefer to chunk the tasks by chapter and then add a reminder for what needs to be reviewed in every chapter (see the upper left-hand corner of the picture) as well as a note about what is coming next (see the right-hand side which mentions citations and permissions). This keeps me on track and allows me to focus on each task within the larger project in an organized fashion.

I have also adapted this layout for a semester to-do list (Figure 2.7). For that topic, the categories might be "to do," "to create," "to plan," "to train," and "to troubleshoot." Under each of these, I then list subcategories of tasks. Delineating them into these categories makes it easier to keep my focus as I know *planning* tasks typically involve scheduling, brainstorming, and emailing, *creating* tasks typically

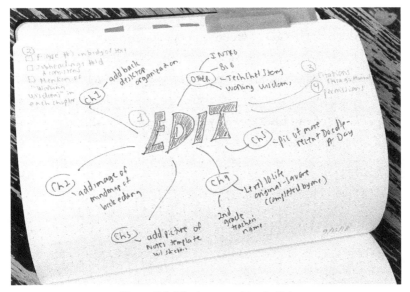

Figure 2.6. Mind-mapped to-do list

require more time and few interruptions, and *troubleshoot* tasks require me to meet with or call someone. There are multiple benefits of a mind-mapped list over a traditional linear one:

- **Mental Energy:** By writing down and then chunking the tasks, I have a better feel for which ones can be done together or require the same type of mental energy.

- **Micro Lists:** Seeing everything grouped in one place also makes it easier to turn this macro list into a more manageable daily micro to-do list.

- **Measured Focus:** In a mind-mapped version, you can see the areas of the map on which you have spent more of your time (e.g., perhaps you have completed all the things "to create" but none of the things to "troubleshoot").

- **Mindful Productivity:** You also get a real sense for your productivity because you don't create a new mind map until you have crossed off most everything from the list. Traditional to-do lists typically get rewritten when they get too messy. In delaying the rewrite-when-messy phenomenon, you add a real dose of mindfulness, as you can see all the things you have accomplished in a semester or year.

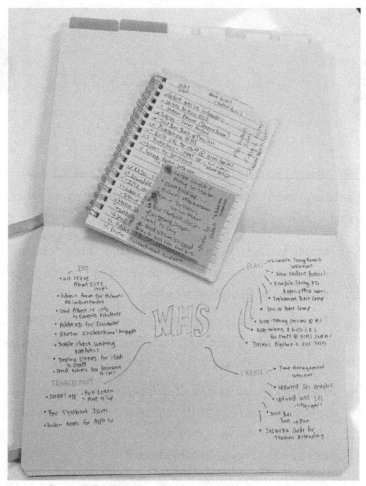

Figure 2.7. A Semester mind-mapped list in my planner

2.3b Micro and Macro To-Do Lists

Learners will typically be able to make a list of everything but then get stuck with prioritizing tasks. I interviewed multiple professionals about their personal practices for managing time, and many of them used a similar practice to the one I use. All these ideas are shared in the "Working Wisdoms" section of this book. Here's a how I use a brain dump to create macro and micro to-do lists:

On Friday before the end of the school day, I look at my planner and my Google Calendar and work through this process:

- Write down everything that is coming up or that needs to be done.

- Jot down anything that will carry over or migrate from the previous to-do list (anything I didn't finish).

- Highlight pressing matters (things that absolutely must be done first). This is my macro list.

- Make a micro list of things I need to do tomorrow or perhaps the next evening.

I repeat this process again for my personal and professional weekly to-do list on Sunday nights.

2.3c Flow-Charting an Event

For large-scale events or recurring projects, it is wise to create a to-do list so you don't forget a step. Students may not encounter these as often as they move from class to class and teacher to teacher every year. This idea is helpful to map out a process you must complete annually or a process a student needs to complete that may need some guidance and that has a particular sequence to it. Unless you happen to have an event planner with an ear piece and a clipboard to manage the details of your events, you'll want—need—this list. When I am planning our annual iPad Base Camps, I must remember to reserve the space, contact the teachers, and remind the students to bring charged iPads. Every one of those tasks is on a flow chart I have created (Figure 2.8) for that event. Even if you have your system down and can put on your events each time so they function like a well-oiled machine, having a recorded plan is helpful to those who will be working with you.

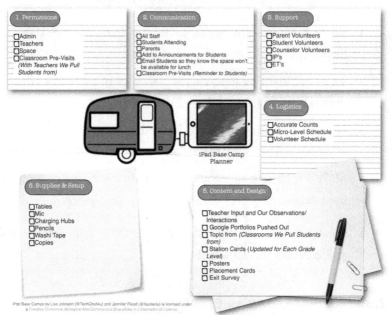

Figure 2.8: iPad base camp flow chart created using Pages, Canva, and Noun Project

2.3d Productivity Bingo

Productivity Bingos is a system I adapted from examples I'd seen by @lalalauren.creates on Instagram. Let's face it: Too often our to-do list is full of things we don't want to do but need to be done. When we procrastinate on those things, we end up in a pickle. Productivity bingo is a way to gamify the process of getting things done. You create a bingo board for a duration of time (e.g., a week, month, or six-week period) and fill in each square with a task or project. This allows you to choose where on the board you would like to place tasks. The fact that you get to decide where to place the task adds a layer of strategy when you put a simple task (something you enjoy doing) in each of the corners. Those tasks are easy to mark off and set you up for getting a four corners bingo quickly so you can win a prize. Oh, I didn't mention there were prizes, did I? Why, yes, there are! Determine the rewards of the game from the onset, (e.g., your bingo earns you thirty minutes of Netflix or a snack, or whatever floats your boat). *Mmmm*, perhaps a root beer float? When I asked students about ways they liked to take breaks or reward themselves, they shared ideas like playing a timed round of a game or checking their social media.

The first time I created a productivity bingo, I loaded it up with too many difficult tasks and then ended up not doing so well. I consequently ended up feeling badly about myself. Lesson learned. Now I throw in a few easy ones to get the ball rolling. You can also do something like this to encourage health and wellness. Recently I created a self-care bingo that included items like a neighborhood walk, going to a museum, an analog evening, browsing a bookstore, etc. After all, sometimes to-do lists can be fun.

When I did this with students, I reminded them to build in prizes (i.e., positive reinforcement). And if you are concerned students will find it difficult to fill in twenty-five squares, you might be surprised. One student quickly started jotting down the *To Kill a Mockingbird* chapters she had to annotate, Spanish reviews to be completed, and math practices to be finished. Of all the planning/productivity activities I teach my students, I find this one to be the most informative. Students will fill in squares with tasks like "buy mice food," "clean out mice cage," "walk the dog," "do the laundry," "find a job," "mow the lawn." You really learn a lot about your students with an activity like this. A great time to try out productivity bingo is right before finals, as students are under a lot of stress, and this is a way to do a brain dump and get everything that needs to be done in one place.

Figure 2.9: Productivity Bingo for winter break featuring sticker from @stampedandsealed on Instagram

Another thing to consider when making your productivity bingo is to avoid making any of the individual tasks too hefty. When I was working on this book, I created a bingo card (Figure 2.9) that had a few squares that said, "write one thousand words." The best thing you can do is make these to-do items measurable and quantifiable: Read one chapter, finish ten math problems, study fifteen Spanish words, play the flute for thirty minutes—you get the idea.

2.3e To-Do Lists for Good

All these strategies to break down projects and processes are eventually creating a working to-do list. I also realize that all these examples I have shared are analog. That is intentional for two reasons: First, because these practices can be adapted to a variety of digital tools, and second . . . try as I might, *for me*, digital to-do lists just don't work. What is important is to figure out what systems work well for you and your students and which ones don't so you aren't setting yourself up for failure by choosing the wrong tool. I need a whiteboard for my projects and to-do lists rather than using a tool like Trello or Google Keep. It is simple and visible, and it seems easier to use something that is four steps away and always visible versus something that is four clicks away and only visible when I boot up my computer or phone. Interestingly, every tech company I tour has a whiteboard in their office and/or meeting room. That's a truly interesting dichotomy if you ask me.

I did find one awesome use for a digital collaborative to-do list tool: Wunderlist. I have started using it to support my fellow colleagues, which is probably one of my favorite projects of all time. After all, if you are just going to create a new account to a new tool and load it up with stuff you don't want to do anyway, what is the point? So we used Wunderlist to send each other compliments and positive affirmations and observations (Figure 2.10), and we use it to this day. We actually borrowed heavily from Angela Maeirs' "you matter" stems.[2]

Figure 2.10: Wunderlist with my colleague Jennifer Flood using "You Matter" prompts from Angela Maiers

2.4 Proactively Managing Time

Calendars, bullet journals, planners, mind-mapped to-do lists, and productivity bingo cards are all helpful tools. They seem like they should be easy enough for any learner to implement. I have learned, however, that far too often, what I think is and/or should be obvious to students rarely is. For some students, setting up or using these tools can still seem too overwhelming if they haven't mastered some essential skills first. And even if they have mastered the skills, they may need some scaffolding, some reminders, and perhaps even a sample template.

In my research into "what works and why" regarding productivity and time management, I discovered that no matter what book I read, TED Talk I watched, or article I surfed, the driving concepts behind successful time management and actually getting things done are goal-setting, prioritizing time, breaking down tasks, and knowing yourself. We will dig deeper into goal-setting in Chapter 4 and knowing yourself in Chapter 5, but for the remainder of this chapter, I want to tackle prioritizing time and dig even deeper into breaking down tasks.

2.4a Time-Management Form

Ideally, students should be realistic about their time from the starting block. One way to do this is to provide a time management-form for students when they are signing up for courses. Figure 2.11 is a time management-form I adapted from the sample found in *Overloaded and Underprepared: Strategies for Stronger Schools and Healthy, Successful Kids*. It serves as a companion to the Hours of HW per Week guide, which each teacher has completed. The guide highlights the average number of hours outside of class each course maintains. The idea is to teach students that there are no more than 168 hours a week and to consider this when selecting courses and marrying this to existing commitments like family, job, sports, hobbies, volunteer work, etc.

TIME MANAGEMENT FORM

For the categories below that apply to you, please enter the hours per week that you will spend on that class or activity outside of school. Calculate your total weekly hours. Once your form is complete, please share it with your parent(s)/guardian(s).

SCHOOL WORK			
School (for most students, this will be 36.5 = 5 days x 7.5 hours)	Est. Min Time (hours)	Est. Max Time (hours)	Est. Avg. Hours/ Week
ENGLISH			
SOCIAL STUDIES			
MATH			
SCIENCE			
LANGUAGE			
ELECTIVES			
TOTAL			

DAILY LIVING ACTIVITIES	
	Est. Avg, Hours/Week
SLEEP	
NECESSITIES (Eating, Showering, Chores)	
FAMILY TIME	
FREE TIME (Friends, Phone, Social Media, Internet, Video Games, Reading, Etc…)	
COMMUTING & TRAVELING	
TOTAL	

EXTRACURRICULARS			
	Est. Min Time (hours)	Est. Max Time (hours)	Est. Avg. Hours/ Week
PAID JOB			
HOBBIES/INTERESTS			
COMMUNITY SERVICE			
SPORTS			
CLUBS			
MUSIC/ PERFORMANCES			
TOTAL			

American Academy of Pediatrics recommends 8-10 hours of sleep per night.

WEEKLY TOTAL	
SCHOOL WORK	
EXTRACURRICULARS	
DAILY LIVING ACTIVITIES	
YOUR TOTAL	

YOUR TOTAL HOURS = _____ of 168 hours**

**Maximum Possible Hours per Week (7 days x 24 hours) = 168

17

Figure 2.11: Homework form for scheduling created with Pages, Canva, and Noun Project and based on an example featured in *"Overloaded and Underprepared"* book.

2.4b Custom Calendar Template

I am not ashamed to tell you I have developed a habit of stalking people who have cool ways to manage their days. While sitting in a curriculum-planning meeting, for example, I noticed that our director of humanities had these blue half sheets of paper that looked like weekly calendars but had places for different types of notes like "projects this month," "people to contact," "meeting agenda items," etc. Naturally I shimmied a little closer to her during a break, cocked my head with a Cheshire grin, and inquired as to what they were. She was happy to share her system, and I loved the idea so much that I asked her if she could send me the templates. She has been using this system for many years, so she sent me multiple versions. I looked at each and created a one-size-fits-all mashup template (Figure 2.12).

On the back, I included a list of time management and planning questions. When it was ready to use, I sent it to my school's academic interventionist to try with his students. A week later, he stopped me in the hall to tell me how much his students loved it and how they really appreciated the questions on the back. The questions often tie to topics he discusses with students when they meet with him, but by the time they leave his office, they have forgotten the plan. (I can totally relate! I can't seem to remember more than three navigational verbal directions, so I am in the same boat.) The questions helped jog their memory. He went on to tell me the students loved being able to visualize the week in advance and having the separate boxes to draw attention to the priority items.

The questions on the planning template are designed to get students thinking about what's most important on their calendar. The more they think about tasks that happen outside of school, upcoming tasks, and planning, the more they can prioritize their activities and personalize time management tools so the calendar or planner

THINGS TO DO

PRIORITY ITEMS	ANYTIME THIS WEEK

WEEK:

MONDAY	TUESDAY	WEDNESDAY	THURSDAY	FRIDAY

UPCOMING TESTS and PROJECTS

WEEKEND	NEXT WEEK

THINGS TO CONSIDER

PLANNING
- What events/commitments outside of school do I have (e.g., clubs, doctor's appointments, outings)?
- What events/commitments do I have that are reoccurring (e.g., practice, club, etc...)
- What classes do I need to study for daily? How much time do I need to set aside?
- What tests and projects do I have coming up?
- What group projects do I have coming up? What role do I have? Will we meet outside of school?
- What missing assignments do I have?
- What tasks or deadlines are fixed and which ones are flexible?
- What events need to be completed this month? this week? or today? (today vs tonight)? Do they have an expiration date?
- What are all the micro or sub lists for this task or project?
- Could my tasks be divided into categories (e.g., personal, school, club/organization)?

PERSONAL
- Is there someone I could ask for help with this (teacher, peer, etc...)?
- What tasks are high vs. low impact? high vs. low need? high vs. low focus? high vs. low complexity? high vs low priority? high vs. low effort?
- How long do I think each task will take?
- Do I have all the resources to complete this analog or digital task (e.g., textbook, files, device, art supplies)?
- At what time during the day/night do I feel most awake?
- How could I reward myself for completing these tasks?

MONTHLY CALENDAR

APRIL 2018

MON	TUES	WED	THURS	FRI	SAT	SUN
						4/1
4/2	4/3	4/4	4/5	4/6	4/7	4/8
4/9	4/10 ENG 1 EOC	4/11	4/12 ENG 2 EOC	4/13	4/14 ACT TESTING	4/15
4/16	4/17	4/18	4/19	4/20	4/21	4/22
4/23	4/24 EARLY RELEASE NO HW Night	4/25	4/26	4/27	4/28	4/29
4/30						

WHAT'S COMING UP?
- 5/5 SAT TESTING
- 5/7 ALGEBRA 1 EOC
- 5/9 US HISTORY EOC
- 5/10 BIOLOGY EOC
- 5/11 - NO HW NIGHT
- 5/7-5/18 - AP TESTING
- 5/25 - LAST DAY OF SCHOOL

TASKS/COMMITMENTS

OUTSIDE OF SCHOOL	REOCCURING	DAILY STUDYING	TESTS/PROJECTS	MISSING ASSIGNMENTS	EXPIRATION DATE EVENTS	RESOURCES NEEDED

Figure 2.12: Front and Back of Student Planner I created based on Beth Keith's design using Numbers and Noun Project

works for them. Below are the questions listed on the back of the weekly calendar.

- What events/commitments outside of school do I have (e.g., clubs, doctor's appointments, outings)?

- What events/commitments do I have that are reoccurring (e.g., practice, club, etc.)?

- What classes do I need to study for daily? How much time do I need to set aside?

- What tests and projects do I have coming up?

- What group projects do I have coming up? What role do I have? Will we meet outside of school?

- What missing assignments do I have?

- What tasks or deadlines are fixed, and which ones are flexible?

- What events need to be completed this month, this week, or today (today vs tonight)? Do they have an expiration date?

- What are all the micro or sub lists for this task or project?

- Could my tasks be divided into categories (e.g., personal, school, club/organization)?

- Is there someone I could ask for help with this (teacher, peer, etc.)?

- What tasks are high vs. low impact, high vs. low need, high vs. low focus, high vs. low complexity, high vs low priority, or high vs. low effort?

- How long do I think each task will take?

- Do I have all the resources to complete this analog or digital task (e.g., textbook, files, device, art supplies)?

- At what time during the day/night do I feel most awake?

- How could I reward myself for completing these tasks?

2.4c Project Planning Guide

Of course there are times when students need to build autonomy and design their own time management pathways. And for that
I wanted to share this Project Planning Guide (Figure 2.13). The
handout was adapted from one of my teachers, Susanna McConnell.
She was finding that students don't always read the project packet or
requirements and then miss info or deadlines or ask questions that
are clearly written within the text. So she started requiring them to
complete two lists. One "What do we *know* about the project requirements?" and the other "What do we *need* to do for the project?" The
first list forces students to dive into the packet and hone in on the
major points. The second list facilitates the process of creating a to do
list. I completed the two lists based on Susanna's packet to give you a
better idea of what might be written in each. I also added a place for
students to write down their group member contact info as well as a
mini-project planning calendar.

Whether you provide a campus time-management form, create
to-dos and checklists for your students, and/or provide templates
to scaffold the process, I urge you to dispense opportunities for students to explore these tools and processes and secure ones that work
for them.

Project Planning Guide

What do we KNOW about the project requirements?	What do we NEED to do for the project?
• Individual research is due 11:59pm on October 11th • Project is due 8 am October 16th (No late projects will be accepted) • Project counts as a major grade • Individual research counts as 20% of the major grade • Grade is assessed based on rubric • 5 days will be provided in class but some work will need to be done outside of class • There are 4 roles (e.g. Historian, Economist, Social Anthropologist, Policy Expert) • There are several potential topics to investigate (e.g. Brexit, The Housing Market Crisis in Spain). Other topics need to be approved by teacher.	☐ Choose a Topic ☐ Choose one of the 4 roles ☐ Complete individual research with 4 credible sources and citations in MLA ☐ Create a group presentation or video ☐ Rehearse presentation ☐ Get group members contact info and schedule a time out of class to meet and plan ☐ Upload paper and presentation to Google Classroom

Group Member/Role/Contact Info

Me**

Day	Task(s)	Completed (Y/N)

Figure 2.13: Project Planning Guide created with Pages and Noun Project adapted from an idea by Susanna McConnell

2.5 How to Teach Students to Limit Distractions

I realize limiting distractions might be an odd ingredient to add to the calendar, to-do list, or time-management salad, but if one is incapable of managing distractions, very little on the calendar and/or to-do list is accomplished. I think managing distractions has a lot to do with managing your environment. When I surveyed students, they purported their top three distractions to be social media, video streaming, and gaming apps. Music streaming and email were close behind. I would venture to say that if I polled adults, their answers would not be far off. We also asked students how they manage distractions. Many of them manage their environment by putting their phone on do not disturb or physically placing it another room. But of course, there is a duality to the environment in that it can be analog (in real life) and digital. Austin Kleon famously has both an analog and a digital desk. While you most likely will not be able to swing the square footage for two desks for every student, I did want to share some tips for managing the environment (analog or digital):

- **Manage Your Analog Environment:** When I am working in the bedroom, I must clear off my desk so there are no distractions. If I don't need my phone for the task at hand, I will place it in another room or turn it off and put it in my backpack. If I need to answer emails or write, I tell my husband and boys that I will be working for forty-five to sixty minutes, and I need no interruptions. If I am working in a public place, I have even worn headphones when not listening to music as a physical sign that I am unavailable for the time being.

- **Manage Your Digital Environment:** As more and more assignments necessitate a digital component and/or tool, it is unrealistic that we can just shut off the device. So this is when turning off the notifications or putting it in Airplay (if a task doesn't need Wi-Fi) are integral.

Distractions are inevitable, but providing students with safeguards and a plan seems to be the best safety net to walking the tightrope of productivity. I am also a huge fan of conversations before contracts, so I think it is important to talk with students about these tips and tools and be open to what hacks they have as well. And sometimes the toughest conversations can be the ones we have with ourselves. I recently read the book *Bored and Brilliant* by Manoush Zomorodi. Her name might sound familiar, as she is the host of the wildly popular *Note to Self* podcast. She also offers a weekly challenge that employs strategies to stop distracting yourself with your phone. Scheduling success only takes you so far; we must set the stage to be successful as well. To do that, we must illuminate our digital habits. When I took the challenge, I found on average I picked up my phone ninety times a day and spent upwards of three hours per day on that device. A calendar and a to-do list will only take you so far. Being aware of what you value and how you spend your time are the other factors in the equation, which will be covered later in the book in Chapter 4 and 5 respectively.

We have spent quite a bit of time together this chapter. My hope is that you have found sound strategies for catching up to the white rabbit and perhaps handing him a planner or an iPad preloaded with Google Calendar and all his events. My hope is that you have the tools and ideas to embrace the delicate dance of time. And just to get you in the mood, google the "Days of the Week" song to the tune of the Addams Family. But hopefully these resources and the distant remembrance of all those years of students sitting on the carpet learning about calendars will help them now that they must manage their own.

AWESOME AMULET CHECKLIST

☐ My students have access to all their teachers' calendars.

☐ My students have a tool (analog or digital) to organize their class/course calendars in one place.

☐ My students know how to schedule their own events and set reminders if they are using a digital tool.

☐ My students have a system for keeping up with their tests, projects, and upcoming assignments.

☐ My students know how to determine which tasks are high priority vs. low priority and which ones have flexible deadlines vs. which one's don't.

☐ My students can break a larger task like writing a paper or working on a group project into smaller sub lists or micro tasks.

☐ My students can effectively manage their evening and weekend commitments.

☐ My students have made managing their calendar and to-do lists a daily habit.

☐ My students have access to streamlined project to-do lists and/or can create their own timelines for projects, essays, etc.

☐ My students have tools and processes for managing distractions in their analog and digital environments.

WAKEFUL WHIMSY CORE IDEAS

- **English Language Arts:** Have students design a planner for a historical, fictional, or literary figure. What features will it have? What will it look like? Explain/Justify.

- **Math:** Have students research the features that most students prefer when selecting a planner or when using a digital app planner/calendar like Google Calendar, My Homework, iStudiez Pro, etc. and share the data and findings to provide more streamlined solutions at your campus.

- **Science:** Have students explore the screen time feature on iOS and/or take the *Bored and Brilliant* "Note to Self" challenge and reflect on how digital distractions impact their personal and academic lives. Have students research how technology impacts them physiologically and neurologically and come up with strategies for balancing online and offline time.

- **Social Studies:** Have students create a to-do list for a historical figure. What type of tool would he/she use (e.g., mind map, flowchart, productivity bingo)? What items would be on the list? Explain and Justify.

SHARE YOUR OWN EXAMPLES AND IDEAS INSPIRED BY THIS CHAPTER. BE SURE TO TAG YOUR COMMENTS: #CREATIVELYPRODUCTIVE.

Citations

1. Foz, Denise. "The Bullet Journal: A Useful Analog Tool for the Digital Age." *Medium.com.* June 28, 2017. medium.com/the-crossover-cast/the-bullet-journal-the-useful-analog-tool-for-the-digital-age-d2bb905fbd85.

2. Maiers, Angela. "Mattering IS the Agenda Keynote." *Slideshare.net.* August 11, 2016. slideshare.net/angelamaiers/mattering-is-the-agenda-keynote. slideshare.net.

Research

- Condren, Erin. Presentation at Wild for Planners, 2018.

- Fleming, Stephanie. Presentation at Wild for Planners, 2018.

- McConnell, Susanna. "Improving Project Outcomes." Presentation at Teacher Innovation Academy, 2018.

- Pope, Denise C; Brown, Maureen R and Miles, Sarah B.. *Overloaded and Underprepared: Strategies for Stronger Schools and Healthy.* New York, New York: John Wiley & Sons, 2015.

- Zomorodi, Manoush. *Bored and Brilliant.* New York, New York: St. Martin's Press, 2017.

CHAPTER 3

Notes on Note-Taking

I really must get a thinner pencil. I can't manage this one a bit: it writes all manner of things that I don't intend.

—*King, Through the Looking-Glass*

Amulet: Notepad

"**W**e don't need good note takers."[1] A dear friend and colleague shared this quote with me on Twitter, partly because he knew note-taking has been a focus of mine for the past few years—and partly because he enjoys stirring the pot; indeed, he stirred the pot. My patience for soundbites touted as solidly definitive wears very thin, so before long, the pot boiled over. You should know that my intensity on the subject of note-taking comes from a good place. My passion for doing what is right for our students along with research of the trends in both education as well as the college and career arena disproves this idea that students don't need to be notetakers.

The tweet my friend shared with me came from an excerpt from a book by Alexis Wiggins that highlighted Harvard Physics Professor Eric Mazur. I wholeheartedly agree with the words Mazur said immediately following his dis of note-taking. He said, "We need students who can hold ideas up to the light and challenge, question, test, and hypothesize about them. We need leaders who can ask deep questions and leaders who can also sit back and listen, learning from others".[1] That's true! It's also true that taking notes helps students develop all those skills. Too often, however, note-taking gets distilled to rote memorization and lower-order regurgitation of facts and timelines. Sadly, when someone sees a quote like "we don't need good note takers," the message is that note-taking is bad or inferior—and that is really what gets my goat.

Perhaps a more accurate idea to tweet to the world is that we don't need good *scribes*. We don't need students to make exact copies of what we say and share in class. We have videos and audio recorders for that, and those tools are far more accurate and efficient. What we need is a way for students to interact with the content, organize their thoughts, and make sense of the world around them. Note-taking is an extension of the brain. Blanket statements suck. And seriously . . . I am still fired up over this quote, and I have two paragraphs of distance. I am still charged, but in a good way—a way that makes me want to share the reasons for my love for this instrument of sense-making (i.e., note-taking).

It is common practice to clump the task and purpose with the medium and strategy and forget that these need to be separated. Each task or purpose may require a different medium or strategy. If I were organizing my notes on the similarities and differences of cells that are prokaryotic and eukaryotic, for example, a Venn diagram or a mind map would work best; conversely, if I were factoring a polynomial, I might use the Cornell method, which would provide a column to work out the steps to break down the terms and another column to explain the process in written steps with actual words. There are also notes you take for meetings, notes you take for planning a project, notes you take while reading, etc. Notes taken in meetings tend to be verbatim or summarizations because people need to know what was discussed and what actions need to be taken moving forward. Notes taken while reading could be a word or two that serve to jog your memory or to mentally connect ideas. We take notes in different ways to serve different purposes.

I have been a bit of a Nosy Nancy lately, taking note of people's note-taking styles. I recently met with a vendor who had come to chat with us about the use of her company's product. During the forty-five-minute meeting, I noticed it appeared she was using an altered version of Cornell notes. She had a big column on the left where she wrote verbatim literal notes of what we were saying and a smaller column on the right where she included additional notes. Of course, after the meeting (I couldn't very well have inquired during the meeting, but I really wanted to), I asked what the notes were, and she said they were a form of ethnographic notes, which are like field notes. While you might think that these would be solely related to the world of field researchers, in product development, you really are doing field research about the user experience. She explained that she used the small column to denote emotional expressions (if someone was frustrated or excited) and to notate problems. After she left, I immediately spent the next hour searching Google to learn more about field notes, ethnography, and contextual inquiry.

When people take notes, whether it is the vendor I meet with, the admin in a board meeting, or the learners in our classrooms, *purpose* drives the process and the strategy behind it. The focus of this chapter is academic note-taking, but because my goal for this book is multi-faceted (both to provide you with practical strategies you can use today in your classroom as well as to incorporate tips and best practices from the college and career realm), the end of the chapter includes a spin on note-taking for PD. Like organization and time management—and all the other skills in this book—note-taking is a valuable skill for everyone; in fact, most of the professionals I surveyed on the topic agreed that note-taking with clients and in meetings was very important. Many even had a variety of processes and protocols for creating and maintaining effective shared digital notes and/or agendas, which I share in the "Working Wisdoms" section at the end of the book. But first, let's talk about why note-taking is an essential skill for students.

3.1 Why Note-Taking Is a Skill Your Students Need

Note-taking is probably one of the deepest rabbit holes of all. One would think that because we live in a digital world, most notes would be digital. One might also assume students innately know how to take notes. During the past few years, I have found both assumptions to be utterly false. To get a better feel for the note-taking trends at our campus and to prep for a note-taking session I was going to deliver to freshman, I first sent out a survey to staff. I discovered 34 percent of classes required students to take notes daily, 31 percent took notes three to four times per week, and 31 percent twice a week. This essentially means that while students may not take notes every day in each of their classes, they most likely take notes in a class (or multiple classes) each day of the week. I went on to discover that 75 percent of

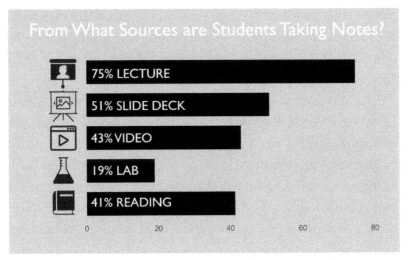

Figure 3.1: Percentages of sources from which students take notes

the content from which students take notes is lecture-based, and 51 percent was from slide decks (Figure 3.1).

The crazy thing is that this is a task students are doing daily with minimal to no training. "Okay, Lisa, but this is high school. Students only take notes in academia. Is note-taking really something on which we have to focus in the real world?"

Heck, yeah! There is not a profession I know of that doesn't take notes in some form or fashion. Think about the doctor who makes notes about your medical information during an appointment. Or the meeting or PD in which you took notes. Or the team with whom you worked to map out a long-term project. *Criminy!* Lynda.com offers a course on "Note-Taking for Business Professionals," which includes keys to active listening, taking notes while reading, and creating to-do lists and meeting notes. And if articles, like "Why Taking Notes Is Important to Your Career," "The 12 Best Meetings Minutes Templates for Professionals," "Recovering the Lost Art of Note-taking," "From To-Do List Hacks to Note-Taking: This Week's Top Leadership

Stories," and "How to Organize a Notebook for Work" are any indication, people well beyond their academic years are learning to be better notetakers. According to the Muse.com, "The Most Important Thing You're Not Doing at Work" is taking notes.

But if you know anything about me, I don't just follow trends to follow trends (except for pretty fonts and washi tape; you can't have enough of those). I wouldn't have devoted these past few years to the research and practice of note-taking if I didn't think it held merit and value for myself and the students and staff members I serve. The more I burrow down this rabbit hole, take notice of those who take notes, and share my findings with fellow educators and middle school and high school students, the more I am validated that note-taking is powerful.

3.2 How to Teach Students Note-Taking Skills That Will Last Them a Lifetime

There are four main elements to effectively teaching note-taking skills:

- Review the Research so students understand the why of note-taking.

- Explore the Styles of Notes so students understand the how of note-taking.

- Survey the Systems that will help learners keep track of their notes.

- Teach the ways of the lecture so it's easier for your learners to take meaningful notes.

3.2a Review the Research

I am a bit of a research junkie. I love numbers and stats and the whys, whats, and whos. It's interesting to me that we often use reason and research with adult learners but not students. I'm not sure why, and I believe *not* sharing that kind of information does our students a disservice. They *want* to understand the whys because they help make the content relevant. When presenting to that freshman class, I loaded up my slide deck with research on the note-taking landscape. I find a framework for gathering and presenting research is helpful, so I have organized it into three categories: the landscape, staff insights, and student insights:

The Notetaking Landscape

When it comes to getting students hooked, explaining why something matters in the first place is important: A few of these stats come from older studies, but I share them because even the Harvard professor I referenced earlier in the chapter admitted that his "top performers could not accurately answer conceptual, application questions"[1] in his traditional, lecture-based, test-based courses; thus, I feel like the issue of poor note-taking is one that is decades in the making:

- 40 percent of students fail to capture the main points in a typical collegiate lecture. First year students capture only 11 percent of a lecture's main points.
- Note-taking can be as mentally demanding as playing chess is for an expert.
- The process and product of note-taking are both beneficial.
- Note-taking impacts academic achievement.
- Immediate and delayed recall is facilitated by note-taking.

- When it comes to test of application, graphic organizers and partial notes were found to be more effective than outlines and completed notes.

- A note-taking template increases the chance a person will take notes.

Students who restructure their notes increase their test grades by an entire letter grade: The article "Why Students Should be Taking Notes" highlights this phenomenon. Many college students were receiving teacher-prepared notes or PowerPoint slides and were then skipping the process of reconstructing their notes. When students restructured their notes using a three-part process (e.g., submit typed reorganized notes, summarize main point of lecture in thirty words or less, and select one important detail from the material in one-hundred-fifty words and relate it back to the main point), they achieved 72 percent correct on questions from the week they engaged in the note restructuring as compared to 61 percent in previous weeks.

As I shared these bits of information, I looked around the crowd—of students—and to my surprise, they were all engaged.

Staff Insights

My goal was to go beyond informing these freshmen about the power of note-taking and to make the skill seem relevant to them. One of the best ways to do that is to share data from their teachers and their own school. Below are two findings from that survey:

- Almost a fourth of our teachers offered videos of their notes/lesson all the time and 40 percent sometimes.

- The vast majority of our teachers encouraged Cornell notes over the other forms of note-taking.

Student Insights

Students are always curious about how they compare to others in their preferences, processes, and behaviors. Because I was just as curious, I did an informal survey of the freshmen in the room (e.g., "raise your hand if you . . .") and discovered that 50–75 percent of them took notes on paper. In another session I delivered to middle school students (albeit a smaller sampling), I discovered this to be a similar trend (Figure 3.2), as 89 percent reported they handwrite on paper, 40 percent type, and 17 percent handwrite on the iPad. I found similar results at the high school level when I surveyed them (a much larger sampling) in the fall of 2018. Now, I have no intention of arguing the merits of paper vs. digital because, honestly, I think that is a smokescreen for the bigger issues: handwriting vs. typing and transcribing vs. sense-making.

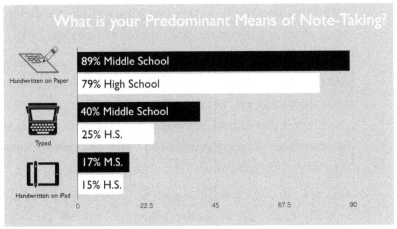

Figure 3.2: Data of note-taking from middle school and high school

3.2b Explore the Styles of Notes

After I piqued their interest in note-taking with my thrilling research and statistics, I moved into the main event: the different styles of notes. Often *if* students are taught to take notes in a class, they are typically taught one style of notes specifically designed for that class' content. Rarely are they given a variety of options and taught which would work best for different scenarios. I explained that choosing a note-taking format is kind of like choosing the right pair of shoes. Sure, there are multiple types (e.g., boots, heels, flip-flops, sneakers), and they all function similarly, but you wouldn't wear flip-flops to a race or heels to rock climb.

Note-taking styles fit into four categories (Figure 3.3): Cornell notes, outlines, charts, and mind maps. Each of these note-taking styles serves a specific purpose:

- **Cornell:** Cornell notes are easy to record and review. They are perfect for extracting major concepts, which lends itself to being an on-ramp to processing info before studying.

- **Outline:** Outlines are well organized, easy to record digitally, and they are swell for recording relationships between topics and subtopics as well as facts and sequences. The downside is that they require additional thought during the class or lecture to ensure they are appropriately and correctly organized, and they don't necessarily work if the lecture is fast-paced.

- **Chart:** Charts minimize the amount of writing, as they are typically organized in similar columns. They are great for facts, comparisons, and relationships. The downside is that they require one to know the content covered in the lecture beforehand so you are able to set up your notes.

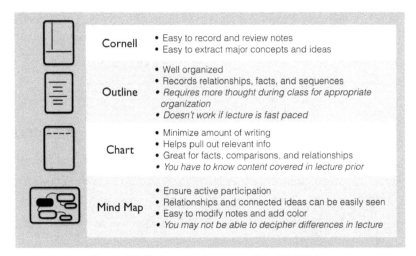

	Cornell	• Easy to record and review notes • Easy to extract major concepts and ideas
	Outline	• Well organized • Records relationships, facts, and sequences • *Requires more thought during class for appropriate organization* • *Doesn't work if lecture is fast paced*
	Chart	• Minimize amount of writing • Helps pull out relevant info • Great for facts, comparisons, and relationships • *You have to know content covered in lecture prior*
	Mind Map	• Ensure active participation • Relationships and connected ideas can be easily seen • Easy to modify notes and add color • *You may not be able to decipher differences in lecture*

Figure 3.3: Each type of notes and the highlights

- **Mind Map:** Mind maps ensure active participation, are beneficial for visual learners, make it super easy to see connected ideas and relationships, and are easy to edit and color. The downside would be that one might not be able to decipher the difference between major points and facts and sub topics within the lecture.

Other styles of notes are worth mentioning here too. The **Flow Method** is reminiscent of a beefed-up mind map. In addition to taking notes, the flow method is about making connections to other things you have learned and adding your own insights. The more I take notes while reading, the more I realize this is the form into which my note-taking evolved.

Sketchnoting, which can be similar to mind mapping or visual note-taking, is another popular style of note-taking. Entire books are devoted to this art form and process, including *The Sketchnote Handbook* by Mike Rohde, *The Doodle Revolution* by Sunni Brown,

Sketchnotes for Educators and *How to Sketchnote* by Sylvia Duckworth, and *Draw to Win* by Dan Roam. You'll find ways to connect with sketchnoters in the People to Follow section of this book if you want to dive into the world of sketchnoting.

3.2c Survey Systems for Keeping Track of All the Notes

I would also be remiss if I didn't go a bit deeper on the idea of **Quick Capture**. Sometimes we have ideas and notes (not necessarily full digital media, PDFs, docs, slide decks, etc.) and need a place to collect and manage them. Some of the items that would be considered a quick capture would be a creative idea, an article or book you want to read, a list of items you need to bring to school, supplies for a project, or a favorite quote.

Since note-taking can range from Quick Capture ideas to taking and managing a semester's worth of lecture notes, I wanted to share my processes and systems. You know I rely heavily on my calendar/planner and to-do lists. But not everything you want to remember falls into the category of events or tasks. Here's what I use to keep track of notes and ideas that fall outside the purview of those two categories:

- **Pinterest—Research, Resources, and Clever Ideas:** This is my one-stop shop. At the time of this writing, I had ninety-eight boards ranging from iPad Lessons and Critical Thinking Activities to research and best practices on slide design. Because I am not fond of setting up a new site every time I want to curate another topic, I decided to create a Pinterest board for each chapter of my first book. That way every time I found an additional activity or piece of research to support that chapter, I was able to update my resource. I also use Pinterest as a portfolio and have a board for all podcasts, webinars, and

Twitter chats that I have done as well as any publication I have written (not on my blog).

- **Notebook 1—Long Term Projects:** As you know, I tend to be a bit of a swinger when it comes to analog and digital. I am not married to either yet strangely loyal to both. When I began writing my first book, I used Evernote for the digital drafts but also bought a Behance Action Journal and divided it into seven sections (one for each chapter). There I would write other ideas and resources that I wanted to include that pertained to the topic of that chapter. This would be like if a student was in a Capstone or Mentorship class and was keeping a semester or yearlong project notebook.

- **Notebook 2—Professional Development:** I think the equivalent of lecture notes for adults would be PD notes from sessions or webinars. I have another Behance Action Journal where I take notes in sessions. I also use this when meeting with teachers or professional learning communities (PLCs) to plan, as it is easy to refer back to and it seems less obtrusive than talking to someone with a screen in front of you.

- **Notebook 3—Reader's Notebook, Bullet Journal, and Goals:** The last notebook I have is a Leuchtturm1917 journal. This notebook is devoted to book summaries as well as lists and goals. If you want to start using an analog notebook with students (or already do use a notebook with students), this notebook would be the closest thing to a writer's or reader's notebook.

Now that you know the inner workings of my slightly analog (and more than slightly OCD) brain, I hope you begin letting the wheels turn in your own mind. Again, I don't share my systems with the intent of being prescriptive; rather, I believe that when you set up your own spaces for ideas and notes, you already have a place for each to go, and you don't have to spend extra time and effort organizing them. And please remember that these spaces and systems could be a series of analog notebooks or a service with a hierarchy of folders or digital notebooks. It is really and truly less about the tool and more about exploring and personalizing a system that works for you and your students.

Sometimes finding the right systems takes a bit of trial and error at the beginning. My first notebook was a bit of a hot mess with orphan notes and ideas throughout. I had no idea how I wanted to organize it or what would get written in it, so there are blank pages all over the place, and my meetings notes butt up to my PD notes, and my list of blog ideas, which for me is less than ideal. An easy brainstorm of all the things you do and remember and write down over a few weeks will give you a good idea of what you will need to have in place. Determining overarching categories for each will help you figure out how many notebooks, apps, or services you will actually need. I will also say that when my office gets messy, it is because I haven't decided on what bucket in which a new topic, idea, or actual piece of paper or item will be stored. Habits are what happen when our brain runs on autopilot and doesn't have to work to make decisions. When you find a system that works for you, it affords you more time to spend on other parts of your life that may not be as well organized.

Even after you explain the why and the how of note-taking, you will still have some students who are not necessarily excited about taking notes. But you are now armed with the why, what, and how, so providing opportunities for them to stretch themselves is integral. For many students, high school is one of the first times they had to really study and take notes. Our biology team noted this phenomenon and spent time teaching students how to take visually mind-mapped notes. Interestingly, 60 percent of the students said they didn't like making these notes, yet 66 percent said the graphic method helped them to be more successful. And when students spent less time copying notes and more time processing information, student averages went up; in fact, even the lower-level students matched that of the higher-achieving ones.

3.2d Teach the Ways of the Lecture

The last bit of advice covers what to do during and after a lecture. Direct delivery may not take up as much time in the classroom as it once did, but I know few classes that don't use lectures at some point in the curriculum. What I am about to say next seems totally obvious, but most students are not aware of these tips.

- **Actively Listen:** Most of the note-taking during a lecture is actually listening—active listening.

- **Use an Appropriate System:** I realize this part will take some time, but this is where teaching students the types of notes and their pros and cons is so integral.

- **Pay Attention to Verbal Cues and Body Language:** If students are actively listening, there should be cues (both verbal and nonverbal) within a lecture; for example, when a teacher says, "an interesting fact is," "to sum up," "or what's important here,"[2] these are all cues that whatever is being said should probably be written down. Additionally, if a teacher is giving examples, repeating what has been said, spending more time on one topic than another, writing something on the board, or using body language (e.g., facial expression, change in tone, gestures, or pacing) odds are it is important and worth writing down.

- **Use Abbreviations and Shorthand:** Students are familiar with abbreviations in texting but very few are aware of shorthand. If students are taking notes by hand, they can't (and shouldn't) be writing things down verbatim, but they also shouldn't be wasting time writing out common words. Also, if they are writing on paper, this practice saves space. (See Figure 3.4 for Examples.)

- **Keep a Record of Questions:** While some teachers might run a back channel for questions or use an online platform, oftentimes they don't answer questions until the end of class or the end of a section. This is why it is so important to jot down questions you have while you go, that way you don't forget to have them answered later.

- **Fill in the Blanks:** Most secondary campuses have a three- to five-minute passing period, so it is unlikely students will

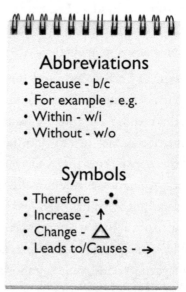

Figure 3.4: Picture of shorthand common abbreviations and misc. symbols

have time to fill in any blanks in their notes after class. But the tale of the forgetting curse (I mean curve) is true, and the way to prevent the curse (I mean curve) is to wear a paper necklace soaked in garlic . . . wait, different curse . . . the way to prevent it is to spend time filling in the blanks you missed in your notes, reviewing notes the same day, and chanting (I mean explaining) your notes out loud.

I know you might be wondering, *Lisa, you said you were college and career focused, but the bulk of this chapter is devoted to teaching students lecture-based tools. Why is that?* Well, I am so glad you asked. I believe we must equip students with the skills and tools they need and give them opportunities to practice. When they understand the why and the how and develop the habits to use note-taking skills, they will then be able to transfer these skills beyond our institutions. Once students are familiar with the tools and processes, they can choose the best tool and process for them and for the task at hand. While one hopes they aren't sitting in lectures for the rest of their lives, there are few people who don't have to engage in meetings, work on projects, or attend PD, regardless of their field.

3.3 Professional Note-Taking Strategies You Can Use

As promised, I wanted to share tips for taking notes in a PD or meeting. If you have seen me in a PD workshop during the past three years or so, you may have noticed that I'm never without my notebooks and an arsenal of colored pens (Figure 3.5).

Typically, notes students take are and should be only used for their purposes: to study and make sense of the content they are consuming and digesting. While I do still want to make sense of the content I

Figure 3.5: Me prepared to take notes at ASCD with my
water, notebook, and sharpie fine-point pens

am consuming during a PD, this content is oftentimes something to
which I may want to go back and review (not just for a test or paper)
and will most likely be something I share with my colleagues or staff.
As most PDs (except for Ed Camps) can cost $195–$1500+ per conference or event, this learning can be cost-prohibitive. Now, one could
follow along with the conference hashtag for free and nab some true
gems and perhaps catch an archived livestream of an event. My point
is that very few people have the time it takes to thoroughly review
the resources rapidly roaring through the hashtag stream. Many
times they rely on the nuggets from their peers or colleagues who
attended those sessions or workshops. I think people should attend
events whenever possible, but if they can't, I want to be able to share

with them what I learned. This focus of sharing slightly changes the way I take notes, as the audience of one grows to the audience of few or many.

I have spent many years refining my conference note-taking process. At first I started with notes in Evernote (to which I now hardly ever refer back). Later I played a bit with collages: I would take a few pictures from the event or the sessions that I attended and would create a collage with them using an app like PhotoMapo or Canva (Figure 3.6a and b). I would then Thinglink the collage with slide

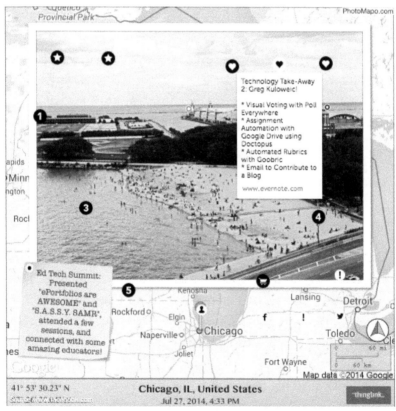

Figure 3.6a: My interactive collage of notes and resources from Ed Tech Summit created using PhotoMapo and Thinglink

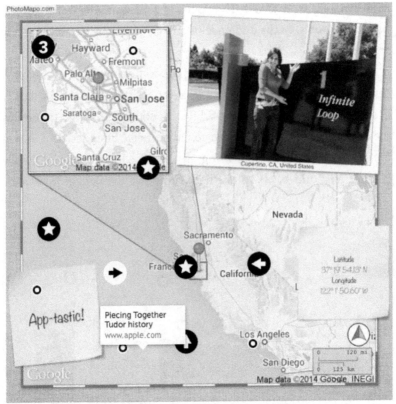

Figure 3.6b: My interactive collage of notes and resources from a visit to Apple in Cupertino using PhotoMapo and Thinglink

decks, sites, articles, text pop-up descriptions, and summaries. This seemed to be a good fit for a while, as it was visual, easy to navigate, and held all the necessary support resources. I also found that the teachers with whom I shared these really liked them. I created seven of these collages over a two-year period and then started dabbling with handwritten notes.

As with anything new you try, the more you practice, the better you get. Originally my handwritten notes for conferences were still very text heavy (Figure 3.7). But I noticed a few benefits very quickly.

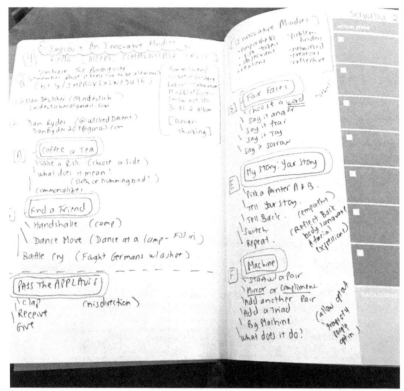

Figure 3.7: Early analog text-heavy notes from SXSWEDU (South by Southwest Education) session

I was more focused on what the speaker was saying (active listening—check!), as I didn't have notifications popping up in my "notebook" or a plethora of tantalizing tabs open, including my email. I also was only jotting down in my notebook what I felt relevant rather than trying to gather everything the speaker said (not transcribing but transforming—check!). Pretty soon I found myself drawing mind-maps and even icons (Figure 3.8a and b). Sure enough, I found that this style of note-taking was not only better for me as a conference or workshop participant but provided far more insight and information to the people with whom I then shared my notes.

Figure 3.8a: My analog notes from SXSWEDU session turned interactive using Canva and Thinglink

Figure 3.8b: My analog notes from Corwin's Women in Leadership session turned interactive using Canva and Thinglink

With time and practice, my handwritten notes began to take the form of sketchnotes or mind maps. The funny thing about looking at someone else's notes (no matter how colorful or pretty they might be), is that they are someone else's notes. As my notes, in this case, were ultimately intended to be shared with others, I experimented with Thinglink again, and this time kept it simple. I photographed the analog notes and then Thinglinked them with all the relevant resources and information (including direct links to sites, videos, Twitter handles, slide decks, etc.). Figure 3.8a and 3.8b depict two examples. My staff really liked them, as they were easy to follow and navigate. (They weren't just random handwritten notes. It is as if the Thinglinks were acting like a jolt of ginseng, vitamin B, and ginkgo to improve the overall clarity and digestion of the notes)

Because I get several questions on where to begin and which way you ought to go from here, I will leave you with a few tips:

- **Tabs:** I bought Post-it tabs for my notebook that I use to separate the notebook for each conference I attend. I then add a label to each one. All my notes are chronological, so this allows me to easily find the notes from the conference or session.

- **Dates and Titles:** In the upper right-hand corner, I always include the title of the conference and the date and the conference hashtag. In the upper left-hand corner, I include the name of the session and the speakers and their Twitter handles and emails (if applicable). These get Thinglinked later.

- **Session Notes:** From there, I take notes. I draw icons, build mind-maps and write down things that speak only to me. Drawing the icons is especially helpful to organize the content. I typically have my phone next to me, and I search for an icon on Noun Project and then sketch it while I am listening to the speaker.

- **Colors:** This gets a bit granular, but I typically try to use only two colors of pens. One is used for my headings and the other for sub headings or info that goes under the headings. I also try to keep it simple because wielding two pens, an iPhone, and a notebook on your lap is pretty much a circus act by itself.

- **Editing:** I oftentimes will go over the notes after the session and add bullets or A, B, and C just to make them a little easier to follow. I will also use the right-hand "Action Steps" column in my Behance Action Journal to jot down tools I should investigate, next steps, great ideas, etc. Really, the Behance Journal is kind of like a professional Cornell note.

- **Thinglink:** Once the notes are complete, I snap a pic and Thinglink them with additional info.

As I don't want to tie my best practices to a tool that may be around for ages but may also go the way of TodaysMeet or Tackk, I want to mention that even if you didn't use Thinglink, you could use the processes of dates and titles, icons, color hierarchy, and sequential editing with A, B, and C in your notes and add those image notes to a tool like Google Docs. From there you could create a table of linked resources mentioned in the notes under the image of your notes from that session.

Through this process, you discover your own style, and I quite agree that is the best kind of ending—or beginning! One of the biggest takeaways for note-taking is that it really is a personal affair. Recently I have become hooked on *The Marvelous Mrs. Maisel* series about a young woman in the 1950s who becomes a standup comedian. In one episode, she began doubting her expertise to craft jokes from her own notes and so paid someone to do it for her. As you might think, the jokes ended up falling flat because the notes were personal and had contextual meanings that weren't easily transferred to someone else.

"Sure, but this is fiction, and you mentioned that you design notes for other people," you say. While I do share my notes and try to design them in a way that is ultimately transparent, these are nonetheless my notes, and while they are better than not attending an event, they are not a substitute for attending the event in person and taking your own notes. Just like a student who was absent from class and copied the notes of a student who was present that day would have more information than not having attended at all, she would most likely not have the full picture, as those notes are subjective and filtered through another student's eyes.

3.4 Tips and Templates

If you and/or your students are overwhelmed with the idea of starting with a blank page, a template can be helpful. Let me be clear: I am not advocating for fill-in-the-blank worksheets. The idea is not to dumb down the note-taking process but to provide a framework.

3.4a PDF Note-Taking Templates

Take a look at the template (Figure 3.9) a colleague created for taking notes at sessions at SXSWEDU (South by Southwest Education) and/or recapping the event. This could be annotated on a device and/or printed. Either way it provides some comfort to those who might at first need a road map, much like a graphic organizer would provide.

3.4b Sketchnoting Note-Taking Templates

If you are sketchnoting on a device, preparing a standard template is another option. Karen Bosch @karlyb does just this with the Paper by 53 app. She uses the color scheme from the conference she is attending and prepares a color palette so her notes remain uniform.

SO YOU WENT TO

 Sessions Attended

 5 Mind-Blowing Moments

3 Ideas for Campus or District
Improvement
(Include ideas for HOW and WHY.)

3 Ways to Grow as an
Individual (Personally or
Professionally)

Figure 3.9: Professional Development note-taking template created
by Kacy Williams using Pages and Noun Project

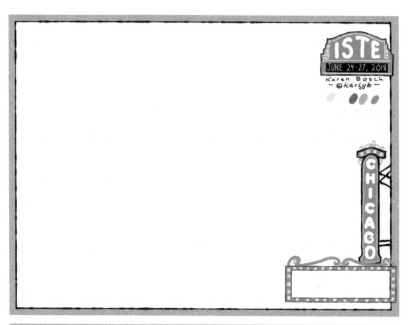

Figure 3.10: Sketchnote template and completed example
from Karen Bosch @karlyb (Twitter, Instagram)
and tinyurl.com/ipadcreate (webpage)

Sometimes she will even create a frame with the conference logo and an iconic way to capture the title of the session and the speaker (Figure 3.10).

3.4c Sticker Note-Taking Templates

Another option would be to use stickers. Blank pages can be overwhelming, and stickers allow students to easily divide the abyss into purposeful spaces with headers. The stickers on the next page were created with Canva. You can save Canva image files and use them in digital notes and/or upload them to an Avery template and print them as actual stickers (Figure 3.12a). For my PD sessions, I created four different stickers:

- **Calendar:** The calendar sticker reminds people to date their notes and include a location for their notes (e.g., the conference and/or class in which they took the notes).

- **Ideas I Love:** Sometimes I make a list of Ideas I Love, or this could be the heart (see what I did there?) of the notes, as we don't typically write down ideas we don't like.

- **Questions:** I often write down questions I have for the speaker as well as questions/ponderings I have that perhaps I need to research further and/or investigate when I get back.

- **Resources and Links:** This is where I write down any apps, videos, and/or books that the speaker mentions as well as direct links to the speaker's slide deck, site, or additional resources.

From the tweets and Instagram posts I received from attendees, I know they really appreciate the combination of analog and digital and the autonomy to choose which version they could use. Figure 3.12b highlights the digital stickers being used in a Google Doc. And everyone likes stickers. I think the only way to up the joy of stickers would be to make them scratch-and-sniff or gifs next time. Oh, there's a thought!

Figure 3.12a: Stickers for professional development note-taking created with Canva and Noun Project and printed on Avery labels

Whether you use stickers, go boldly forth with analog or digital, or decide to immediately teach your students the four types of note-taking styles, I hope what you've learned or been reminded of here moves you to action. My hope is that these tools, practices, suggestions, and pathways allow you to teach your students to be "good note-takers."

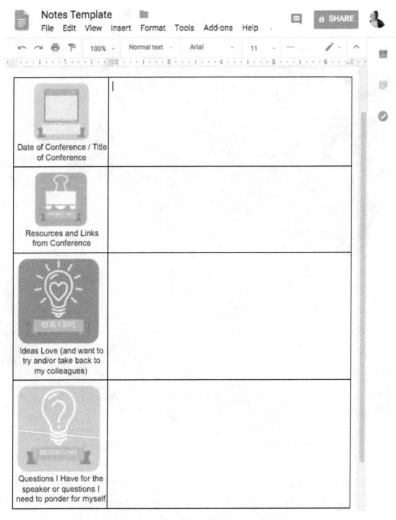

Figure 3.12b: Stickers for professional development
note-taking used in conjunction with Google Docs

Awesome Amulet Checklist

☐ My students know how to take notes beyond basic transcription of teacher media.

☐ My students understand the pros and cons of each of the four main styles of note-taking.

☐ My students can select the appropriate style of notes for a particular activity or project.

☐ My students have a process for quick capture of notes and ideas.

☐ My students have a process for organizing their analog and/ or digital notes.

☐ My students are aware of cue words, phrases, and nonverbal cues for noting important content.

☐ My students are aware of, and incorporate when necessary, a note-taking system that utilizes short-hand and common abbreviations.

☐ My students jot down questions they have and fill in gaps within their notes.

☐ My students can organize their free-form notes with headers, dates, colors, symbols, etc.

Wakeful Whimsy Core Ideas

- **English Language Arts:** Have students research the note-taking styles and habits of famous people. Tim Ferris, Austin Kleon, Marilyn Monroe, Bill Gates, Mark Twain, Pablo Picasso, Marie Curie, George Patton, Taylor Swift, and Richard Branson are great places to start. Note their purpose and style.

What can you learn from these people? What did they all have in common?

- **Math:** Have students create a similar survey to the one mentioned in this chapter. Consider having them determine how often students take notes, in what classes they take notes most often, what types of the four note styles they use most, what note-taking apps are preferred, and what types of analog tools are used (e.g., highlighters, pens, lined paper, dotted paper). Have students share the findings and come up with a menu of resources for incoming students.

- **Science:** Have students research the pros and cons of analog and digital notes and the pros and cons of typing notes rather than handwriting them and present their findings to administration.

- **Social Studies:** Research the four types of note-taking styles and create a guide or a decision tree for what types of notes are best used in a variety of instances (e.g., a character analysis, a fast-paced lecture, a timeline of historical events, etc.). Discuss the similarities and differences of the types of notes and notebooks within each grade level and/or content area. What types of strategies and organization make sense for interactive science journals but maybe not for a writer's notebook? Can students come up with a list of best practices and strategies for the note-taking style in each content area? Are there certain best practices and strategies that are universal?

SHARE YOUR OWN EXAMPLES AND IDEAS INSPIRED BY THIS CHAPTER. BE SURE TO TAG YOUR COMMENTS: #CREATIVELYPRODUCTIVE.

Citations

1. Wiggins, Alexis. *The Best Class Your Never Taught*. Alexandria: Virgina, ASCD, 2017.

2. Georgakis, Angelos. How to take good notes. Kentucky: CreateSpace Independent Publishing Platform, 2017.

Research

- Andrew D. Katayama and Daniel H. Robinson. 2000. "Getting Students 'Partially' Involved in Note-Taking Using Graphic Organizers." *The Journal of Experimental Education*, 68:2, 119-133, DOI: 10.1080/00220970009598498.

- California Polytechnic State University. 2018. "Note Taking Systems | Academic Skills Center (ASC)." Academic Skills Center (ASC). asc. calpoly.edu/ssl/notetakingsystems.

- Compean, Jackie and White, Allyson. "Biology: Visual Notes." Symposium at Westlake High School, 2015.

- DeZure, Deborah; Kaplan, Matthew and Deerman, Martha. "Research on Student Notetaking: Implications For Faculty And Graduate Student Instructors." Dept.math.lsa.umich.edu. dept.math.lsa.umich. edu/~krasny/math156_crlt.ps.

- Dov Cohen, Emily Kim, Jacinth Tan and Mary-Ann Winkelmes (2013) A Note-Restructuring Intervention Increases Students' Exam Scores, College Teaching, 61:3, 95-99, DOI: 10.1080/87567555.2013.793168.

- Kenneth A. Kiewra. "Investigating Notetaking and Review: A Depth of Processing Alternative." *Educational Psychologist*, 20:1, 23-32, DOI: 10.1207/s15326985ep2001_4.

- Kiewra, K. A., Benton, S. L., and Lewis, L. B. "Qualitative aspects of notetaking and their relationship with information-processing ability and academic achievement." *Journal of Instructional Psychology*, 14(3), 110-117.

- Martin, Hampton. www2.port.ac.uk/media/contacts-and-departments/ student-support-services/ask/downloads/Helpful-abbreviations-for-speedy-note-taking.pdf.

- Maryellen Weimer, PhD. "Why Students Should Be Taking Notes." *Faculty Focus | Higher Ed Teaching & Learning*. February 20, 2015. facultyfocus.com/articles/teaching-and-learning/ students-taking-notes.

- Matsudaira, Kate. "The Ultimate Guide to Note-Taking." *kate{mats}*. July 27, 2015. katemats.com/guide-to-note-taking.

- Oxford Learning. "How To Take Study Notes: 5 Effective Note Taking Methods." *Oxford Learning.* oxfordlearning. com/5-effective-note-taking-methods.

- "Effective Listening and Notetaking," *North Shore Community College*, northshore.edu/support_center/pdf/listen_notes.pdf. n.d.

- "Note-taking Abbreviations: Writing Centre Learning Guide." *University of Adelaide Writing Centre.* 2014. adelaide.edu.au/writingcentre/sites/ default/files/docs/learningguide-notetakingabbreviations.pdf.

- "Abbreviations and Symbols for Notetaking." University of Redlands. June 18, 2015. redlands.edu/globalassets/depts/student-affairs/ academic-success/skills-worksheets/1abbreviations_and_symbols_ updated_2015.pdf.

- "Five Notetaking Methods." *University of Redlands.* October 8, 2010. Gvsu.edu. gvsu.edu/cms4/asset/91D2F15F-DAF4-C2F7-B659ECCACE9E7375/1five_methods_of_notetaking.docx_ updated_7-09.pdf.

- Watkins, Ryan, Michael Corry, William Dardick, and Julie Stella. "Note-Taking Habits of Online Students: Value, Quality, and Support." Quarterly Review of Distance Education 16, no. 3 (January 1, 2015): 1– 12. search.ebscohost.com/login.aspx?direct=true&db=eric&AN=EJ1 143760&site=ehost-live.

- Weiland, Andrea, and Steven J. Kingsbury. *Journal of Educational Research,* 72, no. 4 (March 1979). search.ebscohost.com/login.aspx?dir ect=true&db=tfh&AN=5007243&site=ehost-live.

Part 2

Ideas to Help You Grow

Chapter 4

Goal Setting and Habit Tracking

Would you tell me, please, which way
I ought to go from here?
—Alice, *Alice's Adventures in Wonderland*

That depends a good deal on where
you want to get to.
—Cheshire Cat, *Alice's Adventures in Wonderland*

Amulet: Compass

There is a lesser-known Blue October song titled "Define the Trail." In that song, Justin sings, "define the trail that I'm supposed to lead /You'll find that I rollercoaster everything."[1] That song sticks with me not only because I love the lyrics, the melody, and an acoustic set by Justin Furstenfeld but because it holds universal truth. Goals are easy to set and oftentimes hard to achieve. The reason being is that too often we set goals without really sitting down and assessing our values and the path on which we want to be. And many times we don't set goals at all; we coast . . . or rollercoaster, which is really just auto-pilot with boosters.

My life—with two boys, a full-time job, and a part-time consultant/speaking business—can feel a lot like sitting on an Amtrak train just waiting for the next destination. Time and life speed by. Sometimes I sit back and enjoy the scenery; other times I get up and move from car to car, but changing the course of the train while en route is impossible. The destination is set. And if I realize midway through the trip that I really wanted to go northwest instead of due south, I have a whole lot of backtracking to do when I arrive at the wrong station.

I am a grown adult with a penchant for organization, yet I stumble and fall with the best of them when it comes to setting and reaching my goals. When I take the time to do a goal autopsy, I find that the cause of death most frequently is the result of a lack of vision or poor maintenance. So that's where we'll start. To get what we really want, our goals must connect the dots between who we are and who we want to be; likewise, we must have a plan in place to ensure those goals are met.

4.1 Strategies for Uncovering Your Values and Purpose

If you have ever been traveling on a highway and missed an exit without realizing it, you know that the longer you travel in the wrong direction, the greater the effort required to get back on track. That's not unlike what happens when you set a goal without stopping to do a values-audit first. Yes, it takes time, but I must say it is time well spent in the long run. Identifying your values and purpose—*before* you devote your time and energy to chasing a dream—ensures that you start and stay on the right road. The smorgasbord of resources that follow, though designed for audiences ranging from leading companies to parents, bloggers, and software developers, all connect back to values and purpose as they relate to achieving goals. Some provide variations of a similar exercise, but variety is the spice of life—and I felt curating a vetted collection for you rather than trying to funnel you into a one-size-fits-all approach was the best course of action.

4.1a Values Sort

I love the idea of questions and think they work well in journals, but sometimes providing options rather than a short-answer prompt gets people to really think. If you ask an open-ended question like "Who is your role model?" your learners may very well draw a blank. But if you ask the question and include a list of options, you might get a more thoughtful response; for example, "Who is your role model? It can be a friend, colleague, family member, athlete, actor, superhero, etc."

Leading companies around the world use the site TapRoot® to investigate and solve the root causes of problems ranging from major accidents and medical mistakes to quality issues and productivity delays. TapRoot® doesn't focus on role models per se, but it does provide an easy approach to parceling out values. Rather than gathering responses from open-ended questions like, "What are your values?" the site scaffolds a values selection. You are basically given a list of values (e.g., achievement, caring, challenge, growth, motivation, etc.) and asked to write down or highlight the words that align with your values. Then you are to group similar values together (e.g., inspiration, innovation, autonomy) and choose one word to serve as an overarching umbrella label for those words. Finally, you add a verb to each value to make it into an actionable statement (e.g., focus on creativity). The ultimate goal is for these statements to guide your choices and decisions in the year to come.

I loved this idea so much that I decided to craft it in digital form (Figure 4.1). I took a few liberties with the process and slightly altered the directions for simplicity sake. In the digital activity, I created text boxes with words that could easily be dragged to different places on the sheet. In section one, learners would drag down all the words that resonated with them into the provided space. In section two, they

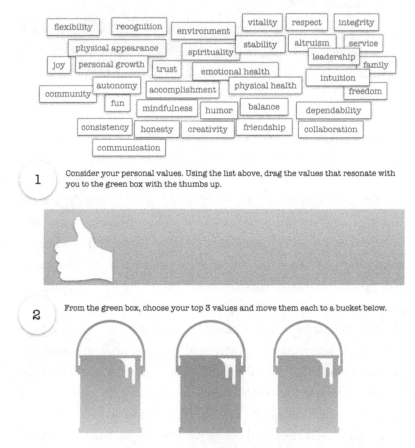

Figure 4.1: Values sort using Numbers app

would narrow down their selection to their top three. From there they could craft an actionable statement that included all three of the words (e.g. I want to focus on being an honest, intuitive individual that thrives on autonomy.)

4.1b Values Tournament

Tyler Schnoebelen is principal product manager for Integrate. ai, a company that seeks to use artificial intelligence to improve the "quality of interactions between people and businesses."[2] In his article on *Medium* titled "Tournament of Values," he notes, "Every few years, I go through an exercise where I collect a giant list of values, virtues, and intentions and rank them. The whole endeavor is a pseudo-quantitative approach to something deeply qualitative, but it articulates what I'm finding meaningful and helps me choose how I spend time, energy, and money."[2] Tyler uses a digital tool called challonge.com to create a tournament.

Although I love the graphic representation and gamified approach, the secret sauce was the deep questions he drizzled on the conclusion of the article for determining the winner of each pair: "Which one do I want to strive for?, Which one do I more clearly already exhibit?, Which one would I wish my loved ones had 10 percent more of in their lives? Which one do I think would make the world a better place if everyone valued it? Which is easier to imagine specific actions around?".[2] Rather than use the challenge software, I decided to create a similar tournament using the Numbers software on the Mac (Figure 4.2).

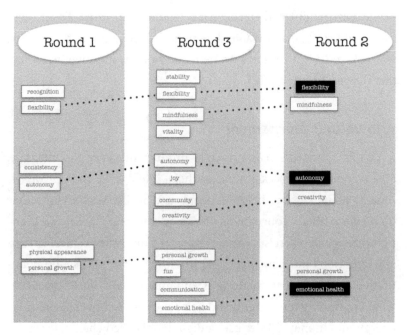

Figure 4.2: Values Tournament using Numbers

4.1c Values Mad Libs Mission Statement

I happed on another clever way to discover vision and purpose with Joelle Charming. She is a wedding planner and designer and offers a unique spin to this process, à *la* Mad Libs. After values are defined, Joelle believes the next step is to design a mission statement of sorts. She designed a letter-writing template (Figure 4.3.) with the goal of thoughtfully considering the elements of a personal mission. For students who are overwhelmed or struggle with open-ended writing tasks, this is a dream—and the idea would be easy to further modify for the classroom.

MY MISSION STATEMENT

My name is _____ and I resolve to live a
_____, _____, and
_____ life.

I recognize that my life is my own, and that I am responsible for my own happiness
and choices. I also recognize that what I value and believe in may not be what
others value and believe in. With this in mind, I promise to treat others with
_____, _____, and
_____. I resolve to start each day with a
_____ and _____ heart.

In the mornings, I will practice self-care by _____.
Every day may not be my best, but I won't fault myself for that. Instead, I will give
myself grace and allow myself to be imperfect.

The most important things to me in life are _____,
_____, and _____ and I resolve to
evaluate my thoughts and actions to ensure that they align with these values. I vow
to nurture my relationships with _____ and
_____ by _____.

Above all, I promise to love myself and live a life of intention and authenticity and
surround myself with _____,
_____, and _____.

Signed: _____

WWW.JOELLECHARMING.COM

Figure 4.3: Values Mission Statement letter by Joelle Charming

4.1d Level 10 Life

By its name, this resource may sound like some sort of gamified goal-setting Super Mario World hack, but this idea actually comes from Hal Elrod, the author of *The Miracle Morning*. The book includes a graphic organizer survey called "Level 10 Life," which divides life into ten categories (e.g., family and friends, health and fitness, personal development, fun, etc.). Looking at the list, you do a quick gut-check and note how satisfied you are with each life category on a scale of zero to ten. Then you design goals to level up each category effectively to ten. Some of the original categories are not as uniquely applicable to secondary students, so I modified them for grades six through twelve in Figure 4.4. If ten seem overwhelming, you could modify the list to include only three or five goal categories for your students or the campus.

The idea is to take a quick in-the-moment inventory of the arenas of your life and list out goals to improve them. While the scale is from zero to ten, I don't look at it as failing grades. These arenas will fluctuate with the stations and seasons of our lives, and it is merely a tool to take inventory of a snapshot in time. As I have been bullet journaling more and have spent much of the past few months with this book, I felt like personal development and my career were in a decent place. So I chose to focus on the other eight categories that I felt have been somewhat neglected during this season of my life. While I know we are jumping ahead to tips for goal-setting, the next step in this process is to set achievable and actionable goals to level up the areas in your life that need more attention (Figure 4.5).

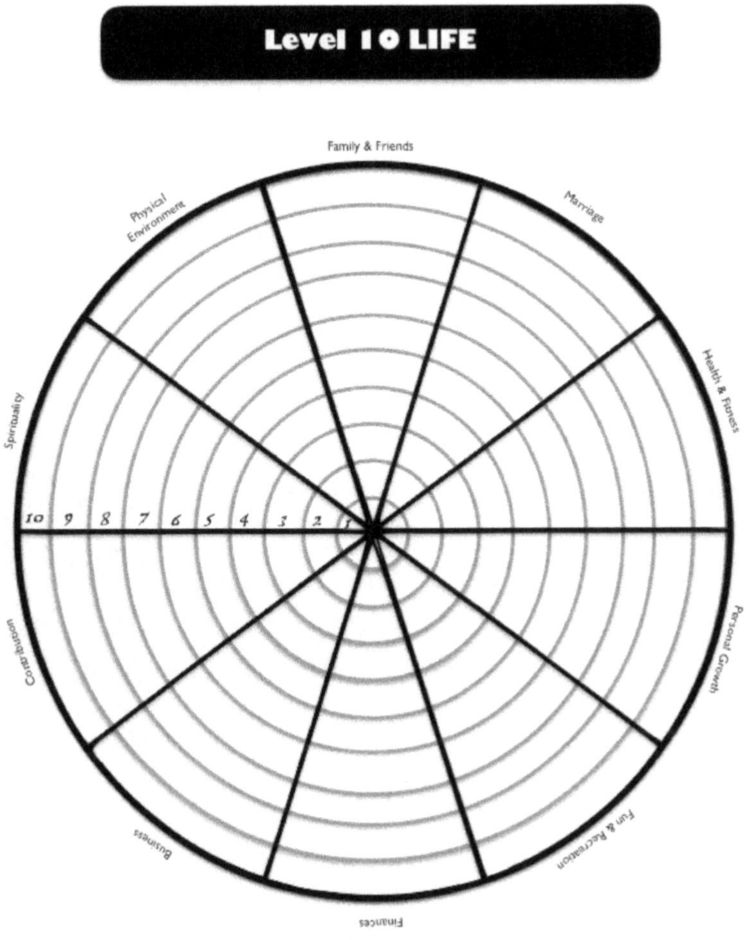

Figure 4.4: Blank Level 10 Life circular template created with Pages

Figure 4.5: Completed Level 10 Life square template
featuring stickers from the Paper Studio Agenda 52 set

Whether it is by using mad libs or a values tournament, the more we look inward before looking forward, the better we will all be. Determining our values is only one piece of the puzzle, but even when we are in tune with our values and set goals accordingly, we can still come up short without the rest of the pieces in place. Those pieces include creating a plan for progressing toward our goals and maintaining momentum. To do that, we must make our goals visible and then devise or select a plan for maintaining the habits needed to achieve said goals, which is what we'll focus on for rest of this chapter.

4.2 Tips for Setting Goals

There are myriad resources, sites, and books devoted to goal-setting, which is why I wanted to focus on three aspects that aren't as widely covered: values, visible goals, and habit trackers; still, I feel like I would be somewhat remiss if I didn't at least touch on *how* to set goals in a chapter about goal setting. So before we dive headfirst into making our goals visible and maintaining habits, I want to take a teensy detour to talk about how to determine what those goals should be.

After you have identified your values, the next step is to determine your goals based on those values; for example, my top values are achievement, contribution, creativity, and quality, so I set goals like finishing this book, reading two books a month, and blogging twice a month. If you or your students are still struggling with tying goals to values, consider the following questions:

- Of what do you want to do more?
- Of what do you want to do less?
- What do you want to do better?
- What do you want to finish?

For me, it went something like this: "Do *more* reading and blogging," "do *less* spending," "do *better* with the quality time we spend together as a family," and "*finish* this book."

I suggest setting no more than three goals at a time. (I went a bit overboard this past year and chose six, which was far too much to maintain.) Once you have your goals in mind, check in periodically (once a month, once every six or nine weeks) to make sure your path still leads to the destination you *want*. In other words, make sure your goals are in fact still in line with your values.

We tend to think of goals from an annual or school-year perspective, but one way to set goals that move you forward *and* are easy to track and maintain is to set them within those benchmark time frames. Brian P. Moran encourages a twelve-week goal-setting plan in his book *The 12 Week Year: Get More Done in 12 Weeks Than Others Do in 12 Months*. The reason is simple: With annual goals, we tend to save our intensity and focus for crunch time toward the end of the year (or close of the academic year). If we set twelve-week goals (which are essentially micro goals), we have more opportunities for high-achievement crunch time than we would setting a yearlong or school-year-long goal. We also achieve more success throughout the year by achieving smaller goals more often than we do by trying to attain lofty goals that have a finish line six months out.

You will notice that my visual goals (Figure 4.6) were set to be completed and re-evaluated in six months. Think about it: Very few people whom I know decide to go out and run a marathon on a whim. More than likely, they set up smaller goals first, such as running a 10K or a half marathon. You can (and should) read about S.M.A.R.T. goals and the specific process of goal setting in other books or in blog posts. My point with this short detour was to focus on an aspect of goal-setting that is often overlooked in education circles. I feel that setting three values-based goals, checking in periodically to make sure your goals are still in line with your values, and creating benchmark goals (rather than one massive goal) is vital to your goal-setting success. Now let's get back on track.

4.3 Strategies for Keeping Your Goals Visible

There is a difference between creating a visual of your goals and visualizing your goals, and as both are important, I want to shed some light on each. Much research supports the idea that visualizing your goals should not be solely visualizing an A on a test or a new job, but the *process* that is needed to get that A (e.g., studying, taking good notes, etc.) or that new job (e.g., updating the resume, polishing your interview skills, etc.). This idea of breaking down the process of a goal into micro tasks will be further delineated in the section later in this chapter on habit trackers. For this section, I really want to focus on allowing our goals to be visual and visible.

If our goals are not visible, then we easily lose sight of them. I am not saying you have to design a vision board at the front of your classroom, but I am saying that goals should be visible so they are easy to remember—and hard to forget.

I am horrible with directions, horrible. I remember one of the first trips my husband and I took as a couple was to New Orleans—before smart phones. While there, I asked the hotel concierge for directions to a nearby restaurant. He gave me three. I walked out of the hotel lobby and then looked at my husband and asked, "Do you know which way to go?" In a matter of seconds, I had forgotten a very short list of directions. Our goals are more important and personal than a list of directions, but they are still essentially lists that can be easily forgotten. A way to prevent our goals from sliding into the ether is to make them visual. What follows are four creative approaches to visualizing your goals:

4.3a Visual Goals with Icons

I created a visual icon for each of the six goals I set for myself this year (Figure 4.6). The beauty of these icons is that, while I may not be able to recite six statements, I can remember images or icons and the meaning behind them.

Figure 4.6: Monthly visual icon goals

4.3b Visual Goals with a Muse

A spin on the visual icon idea is to find an image that symbolizes or embodies a goal you want to achieve. While attending TLA (Texas Library Association), I was browsing the vendor floor when I happened on the Pelican Publishing Company booth and saw author Mary Brooke Casad. She writes the *Bluebonnet Armadillo* series. What you don't know is that second-grade Lisa (that's me) met Mary almost thirty years ago at a Bluebonnet Writer's Workshop in Mesquite, Texas. That meeting has stuck with me for three decades. My eyes welled with tears when I saw her. She had no idea the kind of impact she had on my life as a seven-year-old, but I know I am an author now in part because of the influence that amazing educators and authors like Casad had on me. That picture (Figure 4.7) proudly resides in the analog notebook I used to organize and brainstorm ideas for the book you are holding. It serves to encourage me to keep writing even when writing is hard and as a reminder to give of my time and expertise to inspire and encourage others.

Figure 4.7 A picture of me and Mary Brooke Casad

4.3c Visualize Your Future Self

Even with our goals committed to memory and our values solidified, staying motivated can be difficult. That's partly true because even if we can see our goals, we don't always take time to imagine the outcome of reaching them. In *The Productivity Project*, Chris Bailey referenced an MRI study that intrigued me. When the subjects in the study were told to think about their future selves and then a total stranger, the MRI recording their brain activity showed eerily similar results. When the subjects were presented with a rendering of their future selves, they ended up choosing to save twice as much for retirement as those who didn't. The study concluded that the more of a stranger our future self is, the more likely we are to foist things on our future self and give him/her the short end of the stick. Chris took this study into his own hands and used an app called Aging Booth to create a rendering of himself around retirement age, which he places in his office to motivate himself. I thought this was clever and, using the app, immediately created a version of myself and then one of my husband. And yes, apparently men age way better than women. My husband's future rendition looks like a distinguished silver fox, and me, well . . . it wasn't as lovely. So while I totally dig the idea, I have resorted to just thinking about myself next week or next month and how I would feel if present me adds more to my plate. It doesn't always keep the procrastination at bay, but it is helpful.

4.3d PhoGoals

Photographed goals, or PhoGoals for short, let you share your goals with the online world. Write your goals on a sheet of paper and take a picture of yourself with them, then share this declaration on social media. The inherent benefit is that sharing your goals brews instant commitment, as now others know about your goals and can support you with them. And the cool thing is that you can see how you visibly change from year to year and how your goals may evolve as well. Kind of like an adult version of the monthly infant or yearly student stats (e.g., "third grade, loves *Teen Titans Go*, reads *Captain Underpants*, favorite phrase is "you just got roasted," got MVP in basketball). You get the idea.

4.4 Strategies for Maintaining Momentum with Goals

It is easy to check off items that can be completed in a day, but what if the goal or project takes several weeks or months or years? Let's face it: If you are working on a software release, a new album, building a house, or getting a graduate degree, these won't be completed in a day. Goals die for a variety of reasons. Sometimes they are too lofty. Sometimes they aren't tied to our core values. Sometimes we can't manage to keep up the momentum needed to make the progress we desire. If you give me a little leeway, I would like to provide some context to the latter in the form of a personal story.

I have loved writing since the second grade. My second-grade teacher noticed my affinity for cranking out creative writing stories on my home typewriter. To feed my writing habit, she took me to a local young writer's workshop to meet the Texas Bluebonnet Award authors that year. (Remember that pic I shared?) When I look back on the teachers who made a difference in the trajectory of my life, my second-grade teacher is definitely on that list. We really aren't talking about role models and positive influences in our lives in this chapter, but there is a reason I mention her here. She serves as a dropped pin on the map of my life. Looking back on my memory of her reminds me that I have loved writing for three decades. Writing is a goal and a passion and something I deeply value; yet, even something I enjoy doing and truly want to do can feel like an insurmountable task.

While writing this book, I experienced several nasty cases of procrastination. Reading is one of my positive procrastination methods, and I truly feel like there is some serendipity to the selections sometimes. For the book you are reading right now, the swift kick in the pants that got me moving again came from the book *How to Be an Imperfectionist: The New Way to Self-Acceptance, Fearless Living, and Freedom from Perfectionism* by Stephen Guise. The message, around Chapter 9, fell fortuitously between analog and binary. Much of my book has been rooted in analog practices that have digital siblings, but Stephen takes a different spin on the definition of analog and binary. Binary, the computer language of zeroes and ones, can only have two options, completed or didn't complete. It is in the analog that we can get sucked into the gradients. Analog, by his definition, is "how well you're doing it, not *if* you're doing it"[3].

He gives the example of a light switch. If you look at the task of turning on a light as binary, you have succeeded if you turn it on. If you look at it as analog, you might have a special gesture for turning on the light, or rate yourself on the acrobatics footwork, expert lunge, or fine-tuned wrist flick that you used to achieve light. If you focus on all these things, you may never even turn on the light. His bottom line is that binary thinking allows us to free the shackles of perfectionism so we can achieve our goals unfettered by the concern of how well we completed them. For me, the *aha* came in the idea of binary progress. I couldn't guarantee that every time I put pen to paper (or fingers to keyboard) the words would be epic, but I could make a commitment or a habit to write every day and make some sort of progress—and therein lies the door to the rest of this chapter.

While this idea of binary has helped me forge ahead with my writing, like everything else I have mentioned in this book, this binary practice is personal. We can easily evaluate some tasks and goals in binary (e.g., did I work out today?), but analog isn't inherently evil. In the book *Triggers: Creating Behavior That Lasts—Becoming the Person You Want to Be*, Marshall Goldsmith moved away from a binary system of daily goals (e.g., be grateful, be fully engaged, have a healthy diet), which would be documented with a yes or no because the binary focuses on completion of a task, and analog inherently includes degree of effort. Analog quantifies how hard we try; for example, perhaps my daily goal was to learn more about goal-setting. If I did a cursory search on goal-setting, I would be a success by binary standards. But suppose I had four hours of free time allocated to do this, and I only did a baseline Google search and then binge watched three and a half episodes of *The Crown* or seven of *On My Block*. By analog standards, I would have to get real with myself, and while I did indeed further my knowledge of goal-setting, my efforts were most likely a two out of ten for the day.

Analog and binary are two different tools to add to your repertoire. Depending on the goal, one might be preferred over the other. Now I want to dive deeper into what analog and binary look like in practice and provide you with some tangible activities that can be used in conjunction with them.

4.5 Choosing the Right Process for Tracking Habits

Values and goals are the foundation, but they will only take you so far. From there you must insure your valuables, and the way you do that is with some sort of tracking device. No, I am not insisting you wear an ankle bracelet or a rubber band around your wrist that you snap when you get off task, but I am suggesting some tools that I have found exceptionally helpful.

I tend to wrap habit trackers into my discussions of bullet journals, but they are their own entity. Habit trackers are a staple to the bullet journal world, and they come in a wide variety of shapes, sizes, and designs. At their most basic, habit trackers are glorified spreadsheets that can be used to check off a completed task. Marking progress has an effect not unlike what happens in the episode of *Friends* titled "The One with the Ball." Ross and Joey start throwing a ball back and forth, and when they realize they have been doing it for an hour, they don't want to stop, because they have made so much "progress." Habit trackers are kind of like that. When you see your progress or sometimes lack thereof, that visual cue can be motivating. Perhaps success isn't a finish line; perhaps it is progress itself that moves us forward.

As I mentioned earlier in the chapter, momentum and progress can be ignited and fostered through both binary and analog systems. Just like I provided a variety of ways to assess values, I want to provide you with a variety of practical ways you can teach students to support the process of meeting their goals.

My first student training on bullet journaling and habit trackers was at Fit Fest at Hill Country Middle School. The festival is an entire day where students attend a conference at school. Three tracks—Fitness, Nutrition, and Wellness—and more than one hundred sessions were offered. Courses ranged from boxing, jazzercise, and yoga to food allergies and healthy substitutions for after-school snacks to oral health, CPR, and my bullet journaling course. As I only had thirty minutes with each group, this was a crash course. I gave them a letter-sized sheet of paper to simulate actual journal pages (Figure 4.8) because buying a journal for every student was cost-prohibitive. After providing students some examples of habit trackers, we talked about how to use them to track sleep and water intake as well as how often you study or practice a sport or an instrument. While habit trackers

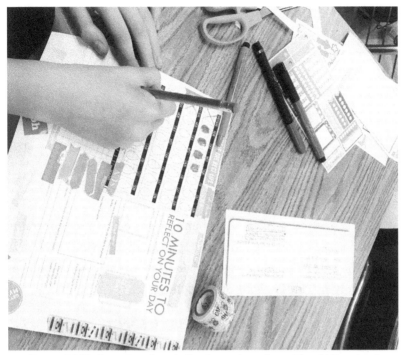

Figure 4.8 Fit Fest pics of my bullet journal session with middle school students using Christi Zimmer's "10 Minutes to Reflect on your Day" (website: christiezimmer.com) and the Passion Planner water and habit tracker (passionplanner.com).

are typically not used to break a habit, it should be noted that they could work that way too with someone tracking if they did not do something each day (e.g. binge watch Netflix or eat out, as depicted in Figure 4.9).

Before we tumble too far down this rabbit hole, I should note that habit trackers are designed to be used daily during a week or a month. While some are highly visual (like the water tracker pictured in Figure 4.10), others are nothing more than a glorified spreadsheet with a blank cell for each day. A more simplistic one is pictured in Figure 4.9. I should also address the granular nature of when a habit

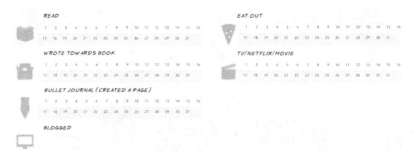

Figure 4.9: My Habit Tracker designed with Numbers app

tracker should be used in binary and/or analog, as it is integral in guiding students through this process. In the previous section, I noted the rationale of binary and analog; below, I want to provide the nitty-gritty specifics to both classifications:

- **Binary:** If momentum and progress are valued over effort, then a binary system may be the way to go. Dee Quine (@decadethirty on Instagram) provides one of my favorite explanations on how to use a binary habit tracker. Normally I see habit trackers as something of which you are trying to form a daily habit (e.g., flossing) but it can also be something you want to do twice a week. Dee explains if you complete the task daily, you then color in the cell (not black) or box each day you complete the task, and if you don't, you mark an X. I like the idea of marking an X rather than leaving it blank because it feels more like an active acknowledgement. If you are only looking to do something two to three times per week, then you would black out the days you don't plan on doing it.

- **Analog:** A habit tracker is truly not inherently analog or binary. It is merely a series of columns and rows. If you are looking to track progress or make something a habit like flossing, then binary is the way to go. But if you are wanting to look at effort, that is a horse of a different color. Marshall Goldsmith offers the distinction between active and passive questions in his book *Triggers*; for example, a habit like spending time with my boys in the passive could be "Did I spend time with my boys today?" and by a typical habit tracker, the answer would be binary—a yes or a no. Goldsmith's system offers an active question: "Did I do my best to have quality time with my boys today?" This kind of question implies a spectrum of effort on the part of the doer. His system is similar to a habit tracker in design, as it is still a spreadsheet, but rather than a binary X or blank, he offers a zero-to-ten ranking that you then average at the end of the week. For habits that tend to be more important or require a larger level of effort than flossing, this is a great way to begin.

Whether you choose an analog or a binary process, I highly encourage you to keep a tracker for a month to get a good baseline before setting your habit-tracking for autopilot. Sometimes we set goals that are realistic (e.g. spending less money), but we are unrealistic with what that looks like on a daily basis or with what a micro-goal might be, so a baseline is helpful to see what habits you need to adjust and by how much each month thereafter.

4.6 Choosing the Right Habit Tracker for You

For me, I wanted to create a habit tracker as a way of ensuring that I was following through on my goals. I had two goals that were positive (e.g., things of which I wanted to do more) and two goals that were negative (e.g., things of which I wanted to do less). If you were Alice, these positive goals would be the "eat me" cakes because they help you grow and flourish. These negative goals are like the "drink me" vials. They serve to shrink our problems by removing barriers.

My positive goals were "read two books a month" and "finish this book," and the negative goals were "reduce debt" and "finish this book." Okay the book is not a negative goal, but its completion was impacted in two ways: one positive (writing every day or every week) and one negative (not watching as much Netflix and/or movies). The latter was not necessarily a goal, but it was integral in reaching the finish line.

Clearly my Netflix obsession was negatively correlated to the time I wrote. No surprise there. With my habit tracker, I had a place to regulate my goals. For the next month, I set a micro-goal to reduce Netflix by five days and increase writing days by five.

An inherent benefit of this type of habit tracking is that the very act of tracking something forces you to pay more attention to it, which ultimately increases your awareness of that habit and how it fits into your daily routine and your short- and long-term goals. And as students are growing older, they can't rely on their parents to remind them to drink more water, eat right, or get enough sleep. Students eventually must track these things on their own, so giving them strategies while they are younger is ideal.

As there was no one-size-fits-all way to set values, there isn't one habit tracker I would prescribe over another. Your values drive your goals, and your goals drive the type of tracker you would select; thus, I assembled three variations beyond the traditional one shared in Figure 4.9 to consider:

4.6a Health Trackers

Unless you are teaching a health class, I doubt you will be teaching students to use habit trackers to document their oral hygiene routine;

still, getting enough sleep and drinking enough water are both bio-logical imperatives, and they greatly impact our mood and how our brains function. Fortunately there are simple habit trackers for both of these. Figure 4.10 depicts a water tracker and 4.11 a sleep tracker. While this would be perfect for a health class, I imagine a math class could also explore these analytics, and an English class could write a persuasive essay on the devastating impact dehydration and sleep deprivation can have on one's social, emotional, and academic well-being. And while I doubt most students chose "drink more water" or "get more sleep" as their goals, they may have chosen values such as achievement, personal development, or wellbeing, which all can be enhanced by being more mindful of these fundamentals.

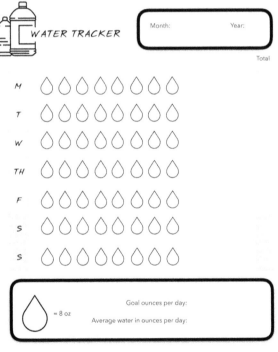

Figure 4.10: Water Tracker example created in Numbers with a Noun Project icon

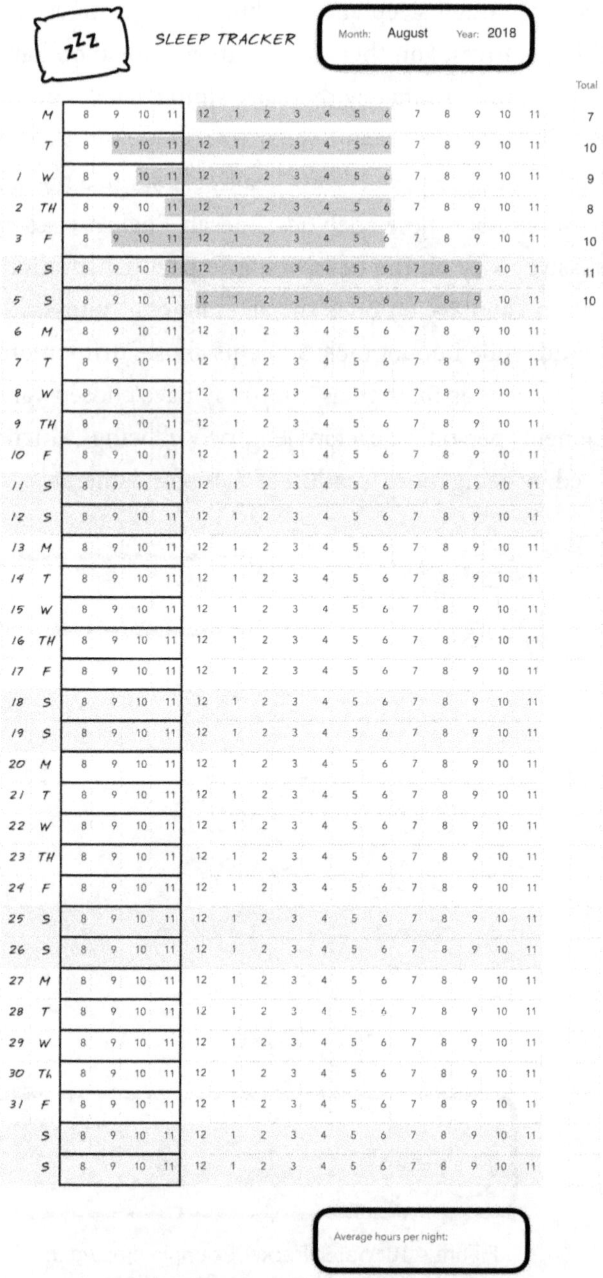

Figure 4.11: Sleep Tracker example created in
Numbers with a Noun Project icon

4.6b Productivity Trackers

Productivity trackers can be used for a variety of things. My favorite is the productivity plant by the Instagrammer @happilyeverafter__ (Figure 4.12). Not gonna lie, y'all. I was initially drawn in by the alliteration, but I really love the idea. Similar in some respects to Productivity Bingo in Chapter 2, it focuses more on time increments. As with most bullet journaling tools, it needs a key. In this case, the creator used green to represent cleaning, orange to represent work, and pink to represent school. From there, each leaf is thirty minutes of productivity, each branch ten hours, and the whole plant fifty hours. This idea could easily be academically adapted by choosing three different categories, such as studying, writing essay, researching, etc.

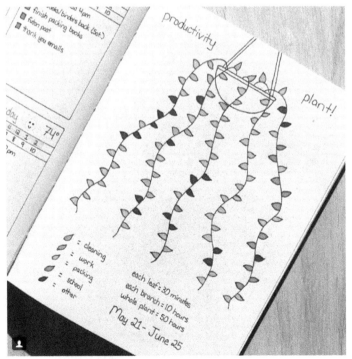

Figure 4.12: Productivity Plant by Eve
@happilyeverafter__ on Instagram

4.6c Mood and Gratitude Trackers

If you thought the Productivity Plant was straight-up Iggy Azalea "Fancy," then mood trackers are pure gold. I have seen elaborate tana-gramed animals like lions and elephants as well as gumball machines and feathers. The sky is the limit! Again, create a key (e.g., blue is sad, red is angry, green is calm, light green is tired, orange is stressed, pur-ple is productive, etc.) and choose an image that has as many sections in it as days of the month. From there, color in the day based on your overall emotions. In Figure 4.13, I have shared the teacup mood tracker from Tracey Collins that acknowledges we don't typically have

Choose colours that represent your moods and create a key.
Colour in one 'heart' every day.

Copyright © Now Paper Goods 2017. Digital file is for personal use only.
For more printables: spaceandquiet.com and etsy.com/shop/nowpapergoods.
#spaceandquiet #nowpapergoods

Figure 4.13: Mood Tracker by Tracey Collins
@spaceandquiet on Instagram (spaceandquiet.com)

only one emotion a day, so she provides space to shade in two (perhaps one for morning and one for evening).

As gratitude and mood are oftentimes related, I have also included Tracy Collins' mood and gratitude mandala in Figure 4.14. This tool provides a space around the outer ring to track emotion and a daily wedge to track and acknowledge something for which you are grateful.

Figure 4.14: Mood and Gratitude Tracker
by Tracey Collins @spaceandquiet on Instagram (spaceandquiet.com)

And if you are feeling super ambitious and would like to chart all your months and moods in one spot, you can start a Year in Pixels in January or perhaps create one for the academic school year or even summer. Oftentimes we are poor historians of our mood or even productivity level over a month (and certainly over a year), so using daily data like this can be instrumental into guiding our actions and informing our goals. Figure 4.15 depicts Alec Fischr @FischrJournals altered version of the original Year in Pixels concept created by the French Blogger Camille @PassionCarnets on Instagram.

Figure 4.15: Year in Pixels
by @FischrJournals on Instagram, Alec Fischer

4.6d Achievement Trackers

Though not necessarily a habit tracker by quantitative data standards, the achievement tracker is helpful when you need some clarity, you feel overwhelmed, or your mind is loose and running rampant with negative comments about your ability to complete and/or excel at a task or goal. The achievement tracker is really a humble brag and tends to be the antidote for negative self-talk. This tool encourages you to list honors, achievements, awards, and accolades; for example, picture the student who failed a test. Rather than acknowledging failure in this one arena, the student might become disheartened and assume they will fail another test or that they are a failure. When this happens, it is important to get a reality check from your achievement list. It should be noted that this tool, like all the others in this book, are good for the gander. And by that, I mean that I created one for myself. When I am feeling low or have fallen prey to social contagion, it empowers me to cage the negativity and focus on just being my best self. There have been many times when I found myself wallowing in self-pity and needing a boost, and this list comes in handy. This list (like all the trackers and goal-setting activities) could also be included in a reader and/or writer's journal/notebook.

As you know, I love my whimsy, but it is a dish that can't be served without a dollop or perhaps a full appetizer of wisdom. To that end, I must note that all these tools are just that: tools. This chapter has been played out to really focus on what matters and how to traverse from point A (values) to point Z (tracking goals and habits). Whether you are tracking tangible things like how much you sleep or how many ounces of water you drink or digging into how you spend your time and how you feel about that, please remember that these tools can't be used as afterthoughts. For impactful change, values must be at the heart of our goals. From there we have some leeway in choosing the right diet of habit trackers to meet our needs.

4.7 Strategies for Padding Procrastination

The funny thing about goals and habits—and life in general—is that we will slip and falter. We are human. We are prone to distractions and procrastination. Having our GPS set for the right course is the first battle; the next is tackling the obstacles. I have started using the Waze app for navigation, and I love it for several reasons. It sees what I can't up ahead and will oftentimes offer me an alternate course to the same destination. It also gives me a heads-up when traffic is heavy, when an obstacle blocks the road, or when I am driving over the speed limit. The app is free, and don't I wish I could find a free version of it for *life*. If Waze for Life were a real thing, the warnings might sound like "Hey, you are going to be tempted to procrastinate in thirty minutes; you might want to move to another room," or "Did you know that tonight your son is going to get sick, and you won't have time to finish those emails like you thought you would?" None of us have that kind of clairvoyance, but we can find ways to mitigate distraction and procrastination. This is not to say that I never get distracted or procrastinate. If that were the case, I wouldn't have completed watching ten seasons (and 236 episodes) of *Friends* in a three-month span, but I do have healthy ways to mitigate the course.

First, I want to make a distinction between distractions and procrastination. We touched on distractions in Chapter 2. These tend to involve controlling your environment so you can complete a task. Combatting procrastination, on the other hand, involves controlling yourself, being aware of what your values and goals are, and knowing what habits, tasks, or things you need to do. It also involves understanding the root cause of procrastination. If I am procrastinating, it isn't necessarily because I don't see value in the task; it is usually because I am avoiding the task—and I am typically avoiding the task because it is hard, or I think that I won't do as well as I would like to. Awareness is important, but at some point, everyone will suffer from procrastination.

While I have tried to provide procrastination-proof protocols with selecting values, goal-setting, and habit trackers, I must acknowledge that these aren't always foolproof. And I also must acknowledge—not sure if it is the ADD or just my personality—that I struggle with procrastination quite a bit. Sometimes I can't banish it. Sometimes I purposely dip my toe in the current and get carried off by it. And sometimes I actively try to prevent it. You'd think after writing one book, the process would be easy, and procrastination wouldn't sit in. But the second one is even harder because you know how much work went into it the first time, and you want the second one to be just as good. Because I knew I would succumb to procrastination, I created a "pro-crastination" list: a list of other things to do if I didn't feel like writing. I know, you might be thinking this is just further enabling my procrastination—but hear me out. The list is composed of things that support the task I am procrastinating; for example, reading a book, researching a topic, proofing a chapter, or watching a pertinent TED Talk are all valuable things to do that still serve the ultimate goal but might be lower impact at that time. You can create a positive pro-crastination list for a goal (e.g. writing a book) or even create a more generic (Figure 4.16) one that includes things that could be more productive than getting sucked into the new season of *Ozark*.

I have several more ideas for keeping the procrastination temptress at bay (because I have a lot of practice). I simply couldn't end the chapter without sharing these tips, because I imagine that you or your students succumb to the siren's song of procrastination and might appreciate some noise-canceling headsets:

Figure 4.16: Pro-Crastination List featuring
Jane Davenport archival sheets paper

4.7a Time-Blocking

I discovered this tip while reading *17 Anti-Procrastination Hacks*
by Dominic Mann. Time-blocking removes all ambiguity from a goal
or task. Rather than saying "I am going to write my paper tomorrow,"
you would say, "I am going to write my paper tomorrow at 2 p.m. in
my office sitting on my floral Ikea Henriksdal chair." When you add a
specific location and time to a task, it removes some of the decisions
and increases the likelihood of follow through.

4.7b Micro Time Goals

I am a master procrastinator. I have known this about myself for a very long time; in fact, while I was supposed to be writing, I spent time shopping on Amazon, checking Instagram, binge-watching *Friends* on Netflix, and building Spotify playlists so I could game the system to get an earlier position in line to buy pre-sale tickets to the Adventures of Kesha and Macklemore tour. I suffer from task avoidance—big time.

To combat my procrastination tendency and make progress on my goal, I set a time span for a task and commit to it; for example, if I don't feel like I can write two thousand words, perhaps I could write for twenty minutes. That felt doable. Nine times out of ten, after the timer goes off, I have enough momentum to keep writing.

4.7c Positive Procrastination Lists

The next one also comes from Dominic Mann. When you are working on a task, keep a notepad handy. When a thought tempts you to distraction, simply jot it down on the list. That way you don't forget it, but you also don't break your flow and current productivity.

4.7d Nightly Skeleton Lists

This tip was shared by Susan Dennard, author of *The Witchlands* series, during an author visit. I am constantly in awe of fiction authors, the way they craft worlds from scratch and navigate dialogue and character back stories. When students asked her about motivation, she offered two tips. The first was to sit in the chair and face your fear, and eventually the words come. The second was to sketch out bullets each night before you go to bed, like a skeleton of what you plan on writing the next day. It is most likely easier to stretch out content on top of a skeleton than no frame at all. This would be like outlining a paper the day before you need to draft it or writing the to-do list the night before you need to run those errands.

4.7e Fudge Ratio

Sometimes we avoid tasks because we think they will take longer than they actually do; for example, if I know cleaning the kitchen will only take fifteen minutes, I am far less likely to put that off than if I have no idea how long it will take. Steve Pavlina, author of multiple productivity and time management self-help books, uses a fudge ratio to not only determine how long something will take but to become more accurate with the estimate. If I think cleaning the kitchen will take thirty minutes, and it really only takes fifteen minutes, then my fudge ratio is 15/30 which equals 0.5. This means that it takes half as much time to do something as I think it will. On the flip side, I could assume that editing a chapter would only take two hours, yet it may take closer to five hours. In that situation, my fudge ratio would be 5/2 which equals 2.5 which means it took 150 percent longer to complete that task than I thought it would. To keep track of this, keep an ongoing list of tasks, predictions for how long you think each will take, and the times they actually took. After a while of estimating your fudge ratio, you will get a better feel for what you can realistically accomplish in a matter of time. While this skill may not win you any guessing games at the state fair, it is exceptionally helpful in your daily personal and professional life.

4.7f Control–Alt–Delete

Behavioral change is never easy. Oftentimes we get comfort from binge-watching a new series on Netflix or indulging in a red-velvet bundt cake with cream cheese frosting. So I feel I should leave one more nugget to support you and your students: Control-Alt-Delete. No, it isn't as easy as the keystroke for terminating an application on a PC. But it does work. The idea comes from Leon Ho, CEO of *Lifehack*. As we have dealt with much of the *Control* portion in our values-audit and goal-setting, I am going to skip to the *Alt* portion which stands for Alternate. If we are ever going to stop procrastinating or filling our time with behaviors that don't ultimately lead to achieving our goals, we must find positive alternatives.

Yes, this is similar to the pro-crastination list, but the idea is not to replace not writing an essay (a positive task) with another positive and indirectly related task, such as researching. This idea removes a negative task like watching too much Amazon Prime (I have been harsh on Netflix in this chapter, and there are other services on which I can just as easily blame my black hole of time suckage) and replaces it with a more positive task like reading a book. If I were just to remove Amazon Prime from the equation, I don't know that at 8 p.m. after I put the kids to bed and plop down on my bed that I would adhere to this media blackout. But if I have chosen another task like reading to replace the less desirable task *and* I have perhaps made the remote harder to find and placed the book within inches of the bed, I will most likely be able to adhere to my bait-and-switch protocol.

Hopefully this chapter didn't leave you with more questions than answers. Your true north is magnetized by your values, but knowing which direction to go doesn't always get us to our destination unless we are in a self-driving vehicle, and even then we will be prompted from time to time to put our hands back on the wheel. Even with clear values, visible goals, and habit trackers marching you closer to your goals, I encourage you and your students to revisit your values and goals (both macro and micro) often. And if you feel like you still need some strategies for revisiting and reevaluating goals and personal and professional visions, never fret; all you need to do is turn the page. I have included many of these in the next chapter on reflection.

AWESOME AMULET CHECKLIST

☐ My students can determine their core values.

☐ My students have strategies to create visual goals.

☐ My students can visualize the process to achieve their goals and create micro-tasks accordingly.

☐ My students have tools (analog or digital) to track their desired habits.

☐ My students understand the difference between binary and analog habits and when it makes the most sense to use each.

☐ My students have developed positive ways to pro-crastinate and/or to mitigate procrastination.

☐ My students can create a positive procrastination list for projects, essays, and assignments they must complete.

☐ My students can accurately estimate how long a task or project will take them to complete.

☐ My students can set macro and micro goals.

☐ My students can set daily, weekly, monthly, and yearly goals.

☐ My students have strategies for revisiting and reevaluating goals.

SHARE YOUR OWN EXAMPLES AND IDEAS INSPIRED BY THIS CHAPTER. BE SURE TO TAG YOUR COMMENTS: #CREATIVELYPRODUCTIVE.

WAKEFUL WHIMSY CORE IDEAS

- **English Language Arts:** Have students set writing and reading goals for themselves within their portfolio index and choose a tracker to track their progress. At the end of a month, six weeks, etc., have students reflect on the process and the tool and adjust as needed for the next month or six weeks. An additional activity would be to research famous authors (living or dead) and to discover how they managed procrastination and how they maintain a writing habit and goals.

- **Math:** Have students complete the productivity plant for a month and determine the percentage of time that was spent on each activity. To spice it up, students could use the productivity plant in conjunction with determining the fudge ratio. To do this, they would estimate how much time each of the four or five tasks would actually take and then visually track them throughout the month using the productivity plant.

- **Science:** Have students choose a habit tracker focused on personal health (e.g., sleep, water, healthy snacks, decreasing screen time, etc.) and reflect on how the tracker and the process worked. A more granular approach would be to have students get the recommended amount of sleep and water in a day and track their productivity and mood from zero to ten for a week or month.

- **Social Studies:** Have students complete one of the values exercises listed in this chapter for a historical or political figure. Students can then compare, contrast, and justify their selections with students who chose the same historical or political figure and students who chose a different one. Students could also research how happiness, goals, and success are defined and how they vary across cultures.

Citations

1. Furstenfeld, Justin. *Define the Trail*. CD. San Marcos: Drive, 2017.
2. Schnoebelen, Tyler. "Tournament of Values." April 21, 2017. *Medium*. *medium.com/@TSchnoebelen/tournament-of-values658f9342e4a5*.
3. Guise, Stephen. *How to Be an Imperfectionist*. Selective Entertainment LLC, 2015.

Research

- Bailey, Chris. *The Productivity Project*. New York, New York: Crown Business, 2017.
- "What is the Level 10 Life?" *Be Level 10*. December 30, 2017. belevel10.com/lifestyle/level-10-life.
- Carroll, Lewis. *Alice's Adventures in Wonderland and Other Stories*. New York, New York: Barnes & Noble, 2010.
- Dennard, Susan. Presentation at Westlake High School, 2018.
- Goldsmith, Marshall, and Mark Reiter. *Triggers*. New York, New York: Crown Business, 2015.
- Ho, Leon. "How to Break Bad Habits: I Broke 3 Bad Habits in Less Than 2 Months." *Lifehack*. August 22, 2018. lifehack.org/678764/how-i-break-3-bad-habits-in-less-than-2-months.
- Karachaliou, Christina. "How to Create a Level 10 Life Spread in Your Bullet Journal." September 13, 2016. christina77star.net/blog//2016/09/bullet-journal-level-10-life.html.
- Mann, Dominic. *17 Anti-Procrastination Hacks: How to Stop Being Lazy, Overcome Procrastination, and Finally Get Stuff Done*. Independently published, 2016.
- Mitchell, Lisa. Presentation at On the Dot See it to Be it Success Summit. 2018.
- Pavlina, Steve. "How to Make Accurate Time Estimates." *Steve Pavlina*. May 19, 2018. stevepavlina.com/blog/2008/05/how-to-make-accurate-time-estimates.
- Quine, Dee. "Dee Quine (rhymes with 'wine') on Instagram: "the one where I explain how to use my HABIT TRACKERS. These have been a bestseller ever since opening my shop in 2015. I'm using the 10 x..." Instagram. instagram.com/p/BdWpZC-FU6Q/?taken-by=decadethirty. 2017.

CHAPTER 5

The Power of Reflection

But it's no use going back to yesterday,
because I was a different person then.

—Alice, Alice's Adventures in Wonderland

Amulet: Handheld Mirror

am not a psychiatrist. (I was a psychology major for a bit, but I am pretty sure that doesn't qualify me to make any official diagnoses.) But I am a student of people and of life. When I look around—at my own life and at the teens and adults around me—I suspect that the increased depression and anxiety in our lives today is due in part to the fact that, as a society, we spend so much time checking on the Jones', keeping up with the Jones', and making sure the Jones' like our posts on social media.

Before the ever-present "reality" of social media, we spent much more of our time with our friends and family members (in real life) or alone. I believe less time spent with family and ourselves is one of the main reasons we sometimes feel so empty and inferior. When you spend time with people—online or IRL—they have an influence on you, for good or ill. If you're with someone who is bringing you down, you can walk away and get a little breathing space. But we forget to do that when we're online. What we don't realize is that social media can be an emotional contagion like secondhand smoke. Even though we aren't in the room with our online friends, their emotions can impact us.

At some point, you must clear the air and take a deep breath of unpolluted mental space. You can do that through personal time and reflection. Rather than subletting your mental space and emotional energy to what everyone else in your Facebook network is doing, plans to do, and has done in the past twenty-four hours, perhaps looking inward is the key to regaining a sense of happiness, purpose, and value.

I'm not saying that all social media is bad. I'm a connected educator and value my professional learning network. What I am saying is that in this relatively new age of omnipresent transparency, there is tremendous value in stepping back and analyzing what *we* think rather than constantly checking in to see what others think.

I recently started reading a fiction series by Jenny Han. The first book (now a Netflix movie) was titled, *To All the Boys I've Loved Before*. The premise was that, rather than tell a boy she was in love with him, she would write a love letter and then tuck it away in a hat box. Of course, this wouldn't do to fill a trilogy of books with enough drama to keep readers going, so—spoiler alert—at some point the letters are mailed off to their respective recipients. The main character, Lara Jean, states that after she writes a letter, she is no longer consumed by what she felt for the boy. As a fan of journaling for most of my life, I naturally resonated with this idea. Sans the letters being sent out to all the boys she's loved before, the idea of writing down thoughts and feelings as a means of releasing them is a sound one.

People journal to feel a catharsis or make sense of the world around them when they are in turmoil. Journaling can be more beneficial than the mere act of self-reflection and exploration, and it has benefits that reach far beyond lessening depression and anxiety. Countless articles and studies have found that journaling benefits not only mental health but biological and physical health as well. One study found that writing about traumatic events for 15-20 minutes a day actually improved the participants' physical health. Other studies have suggested that it can enhance immune function, improve sleep, lessen fatigue in those that suffer from chronic illness, and even reduce the number of times you need to visit a doctor. One study even found that simply writing about test anxiety before an exam improved scores. This can be attributed to the fact that "feelings can act as an impediment to intellectual capacity[1]."

Now, I know reflection and journaling gets into the "hokey" category. Please don't discount it just yet. Your students probably have more interest in reflection and learning about themselves than you may assume. After all, there is a reason people are sucked into Buzzfeed quizzes. At a cursory glance, "Which god or goddess from Mount Olympus are you?" or "Design a park in RollerCoaster Tycoon to reveal your best personality trait" and "Which 90's alt-rock song are you?" might seem like juvenile queries. But they reveal more about us than you might think—not the least of which is that we are curious about *ourselves* and how we fit into the world. The more we are aware of our own thoughts, ideas, and feelings, the more we can harness and channel them to our advantage. (In case you were curious, mine were Athena, Intuitive, and "Santa Monica" by Everclear, respectively.)

My intent for this chapter is to give you and your students activities and strategies that are directly applicable to both your personal and academic lives. In my first book, *Cultivating Communication in the Classroom,* I spent an entire chapter on portfolios and resumes in which I included multiple ideas for academic reflection and reflecting on one's body of work (e.g., a portfolio) with a peer and/or during student conferences. In this book, I want to broaden the types of journaling and reflection activities because I see such a need for better understanding oneself as a learner and as a human being—particularly at the secondary level. We can often answer the question "What do you know about this student as a learner?" but not "What do you know about this student as a person?" Both are equally telling.

5.1 Reflections You Can Use (or Teach) to Explore the Inner Self

I feel like authentic activities and assignments are always the way to go. As such, I have drawn from a variety of industries and products to provide you with an array of journal prompts and activities. If you were to do an Amazon search for journals or journal prompts, you would find more than forty thousand results. Search #journal or #journaling on Instagram and you'll find over 3.5 million posts. Instead of having you wade through all those results, I am providing seven places I go to discover prompts, and I will explain how to use them.

5.1a Explore a Book of Daily Prompts

Some of the teachers at my school have an attendance question of the day. It is typically something quick, such as "What does happiness smell like?" or "What was the last song you listened to?" For me, the former would be "cotton candy," no question. The idea of an attendance question is two-fold: Everyone gets to answer and share, and everyone gets to know everyone else in the classroom. One of my dear friends recently gave me the Q&A a Day: Five-Year Journal. What I love about the book is that you ask yourself the same question on the same day every year for five years. Students can compare their answers to their friends daily, but I think there is something special in the ability to see how your responses change over five years. This would be a fantastic idea for English teachers to start in sixth grade. And I can't believe I am saying this, but a tangible journal would not be my preference for this one. I would do this in Google Docs, Microsoft OneNote, or Evernote, as it would be easy to have it travel from year to year. You obviously wouldn't have to do this every day. One could select thirty-six questions (perhaps one a week) that would be used for the five-year span. Here are a few of the questions mentioned in the journal:[2]

- What are you reading right now?
- What are you looking forward to?
- What is your biggest obstacle right now?
- What's your simplest pleasure?

5.1b Explore a Planner with Monthly Prompts

When I first got my Passion Planner, the prompts overwhelmed me. It wasn't until my second year using the planner that I started exploring the prompts, but I can tell you I am so glad I did. Now they keep me grounded, grateful, and able to gear up for the next month. Much like the Q&A-a-Day format, the journal prompts you with the same six questions every month[3]:

- What was the most memorable part of this past month? Describe it.

- What were the three biggest lessons you've learned this month?

- Review your planner for the past month and assess your priorities. Are you happy with how you spent your time? If not, what steps can you take next month to adjust them?

- How are you different between this past month and the month before it?

- What or who are you especially grateful for this past month?

- Name three things you can improve on this upcoming month. What are concrete actions you can take to work toward these improvements?

Two of my favorites are the memorable part of the month and what/who I am especially grateful for. Too often we get into the daily grind and don't realize there are many memorable things that have happened. One moment I noted was my son getting the flu and my having to stay home with him. This could have been a negative, but we made the most of the time together and bonded while watching a season of *Stranger Things*. I noted in another month that one of my Facebook friends (I deleted Facebook from my phone but not my computer, so I only check it purposefully) had reached out to me in a direct message and asked how I was doing. It was simple, but her connection really made my day. As I jotted down her name, I remembered the importance of paying it forward and being grateful and sent her a message at the end of the month telling her how grateful I was for her kind words. If you decide to embark on activities like this with your students, I would suggest doing them every six or nine weeks, as months don't typically have the same impact on the scholastic world as they do in the business world. I should also mention that there is much research to back up this idea of gratitude as well. And I am sure it wouldn't surprise you that when we asked teachers in a PD how they would like to be thanked, many said hand-written cards and edible treats. Gratitude functions as relationship maintenance and, it is good for you too; in fact, "writing letters of gratitude increased participants' happiness and life satisfaction, while decreasing depressive symptoms."[4] Author of *The Happiness Advantage: The Seven Principles of Positive Psychology That Fuel Success and Performance at Work*, Shawn Achor, discovered that people were able to train their brain to become more optimistic and positive in two minutes a day. For twenty one days straight, all the participants did was jot down three new things they were grateful for each day.

5.1c Explore Apps That Track Data and Build in a Reflection

There are multiple apps that gather data, whether it be fitness or health or usage. After I read *Bored and Brilliant*, I downloaded the Moment app and explored the idea. The app collects data on your screen-time usage. The idea is not that you should give up all screen-time usage but that you would have a greater awareness of it and purpose for it if you had the stats on its usage. When you realize that you spend two hours on your phone per day (fifteen hours a week) and pick it up ninety or so times per day, it may well change how you think about your phone. The app also comes preloaded with the "Bored and Brilliant" challenge and even daily challenges. Day 1 is simply to notice why you picked up your phone: Did it ding? Were you bored? Was it impulse? Day 3's challenge is to abstain from taking photos. We pay less attention to the memory when we take a photo because we know it is saved externally. Day 4 is to delete your most used app. As I had already deleted Facebook, I gave myself a pass on this one. But if I am being totally honest, Instagram is now becoming a bit of an obsession for me, so there's that.

5.1d Explore Poetry and Letter Writing

I love me some poetry, comedy, theater, and impov (in manageable doses). I love it all. At SXSWEDU I went to a two-hour session with Cometry on comedy and poetry and mental health. I tell you, it could not have been more relevant. Their site (cometry.org) is fantastic. One of the activities we did as a group was to write a letter "To My Fear of _____," and the room went quiet as everyone got to work. I spent ten minutes typing "To My Fear of Failure." I share the original letter (personal as it is) in Figure 5.1 because I think it is so important to know that there are many internal struggles we don't talk about and to know you are never alone. What I didn't know when I started writing the piece is that we would be sharing it with the small group of strangers that sat around us. I volunteered and shakily began to read, not making eye contact with a soul. Everyone stared at me with kind eyes, and sure enough, two other women in the group also began their letter with "To My Fear of Failure." A weight had been lifted off my shoulders in a matter of fifteen minutes. Like a good teacher, the Cometry peeps saw that this activity of letter writing was cathartic and impactful. And though we had gone way over the allotted time for the activity, they continued to let others share their letters with the larger group. There were letters "To My Fear of Getting Lost," "To My Fear of Displeasing Others," and "To My Fear of Unworthiness."

Suddenly this fear I had been harboring for so long didn't feel that ominous after sharing it with others. While we didn't get to them, two other letter writing stems they shared were "To the Person Whose Name I Don't Know" and "To the Person Who Thinks They Are

To my fear of failure...

I know I shouldn't be afraid of you. I know I should embrace you. But you feel like a mountain... something immense and overwhelming blocking my future. Or perhaps you are a dark hole... a void... an unknown. You appear when I least expect you to. You appear in a conversation with my husband, in a thought about my child's future, and most definitely when I began to write.

Who will read it? Who will care? Will it be like that last one? Why am I drawn to something that may or may not matter to anyone? Asking why doesn't seem to make the fear dissipate. Only sitting down and facing that fear. That blinking cursor, addressing head on the elephant in the room during a conversation, and acknowledging that you have done your best with your children. I wish we could part ways, I wish I could delete you like I did the Facebook app from my phone in April of last year but the issue is that you aren't an external force or application I can trash. You are with me. You are that nagging voice I can't seem to shush. I wonder if others struggle as much with their fears as I do. I wonder if others experience the same inner turmoil. I know I can move past you... but for some reason it always feels like a right of passage to battle fear... and sometimes I feel like I am ill equipped. Like I am operating on an empty tank and maybe that is really the problem.

Someday, I will be able to knock you down and peg, flick you off my shoulder, but for now you have my ear and I can't seem to silence your shouts of doubt.

Figure 5.1: "To My Fear of Failure" letter written during a SXSWEDU workshop delivered by Cometry

Alone." I should also mention that I attended my first poetry slam a few years ago. A few months later, I composed my own poem about motherhood and a child with special needs (Figure 5.2). It was my first time to speak about it publicly, and I was so proud of myself for getting through it without crying. A moment after I walked off that stage, a colleague with tears in her eyes hugged me and said, "Thank you." You see, the power of poetry and letter writing is two-fold: It allows us to get to the heart of our struggle and identify it. And when we have done that, we can choose to share that with the world. I'm sure you have heard a poem or a song and felt like it was written just for you. This is no different.

Figure 5.2: Poetry Slam poem for iPadpalooza
held at Spider House in Austin, TX

A few of our English teachers have a Friday session where people put questions into a jar and then pull them out. Sometimes it is "best place for tacos" and other times the discussions get deep: fear of not getting into colleges, topics in the news, etc. If you have built a trusting community within your classroom, I highly encourage these types of activities because students need a place to make sense of the world in which they live. And if not in your classroom or at school, then where and with whom?

5.1e Explore Instagrammer Feeds

I am fairly new to the Instagram fam. As I mentioned earlier, #journal is a fairly popular label for posts. While scouring those posts, I discovered @guidedjournaler (Christie Zimmer). Zimmer posts journal prompts and printables. One of my favorite types of prompts is the ten-minute journaling prompt. Her "10 Minutes to Highlight Your Day" and "10 Minutes to Recognize the Good Stuff" (Figure 5.3) prompts give you those few minutes to write about things that make you grateful. What I love about her prompts is that she includes boxes in which you can write or draw, as journaling doesn't have to be purely textual in nature.

Michelle Rorh, @michelleerohr on Instagram shared another prompt, the "Secret Owl Positive Self Check-In" (Figure 5.4). A fill-in-the-blanks letter, almost like a mad lib, is designed to assist you with reflecting, channeling your positive attitude, and finding peace and gratitude in the now while looking forward to what you can do next.

While not a journaling prompt per se, I did see the idea of Doodle-a-Day floating around Instagram. The original idea is less about reflection and more about drawing a different image on a grid every day. The way I went about it was to draw a picture of my favorite thing or the most momentous thing that happened that day. Of all

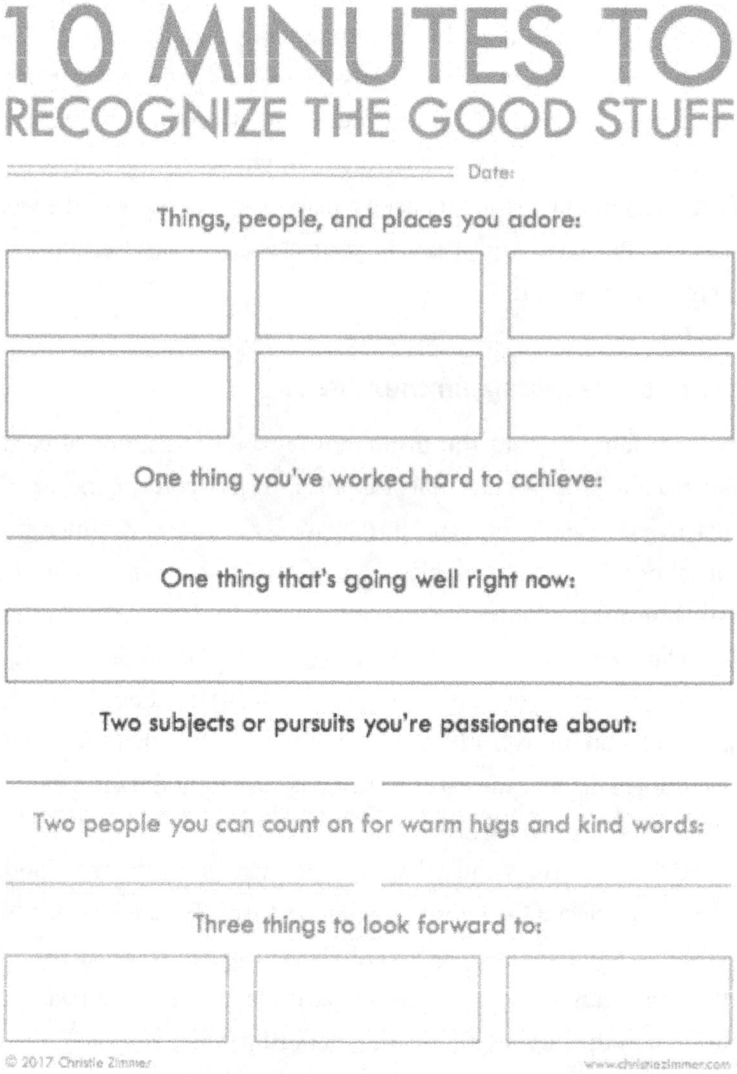

10 MINUTES TO
RECOGNIZE THE GOOD STUFF

Date:

Things, people, and places you adore:

One thing you've worked hard to achieve:

One thing that's going well right now:

Two subjects or pursuits you're passionate about:

Two people you can count on for warm hugs and kind words:

Three things to look forward to:

© 2017 Christie Zimmer   www.christiezimmer.com

Figure 5.3 10 Minute journaling template by Christie Zimmer
@guidedjournaler on Instagram (christiezimmer.com)

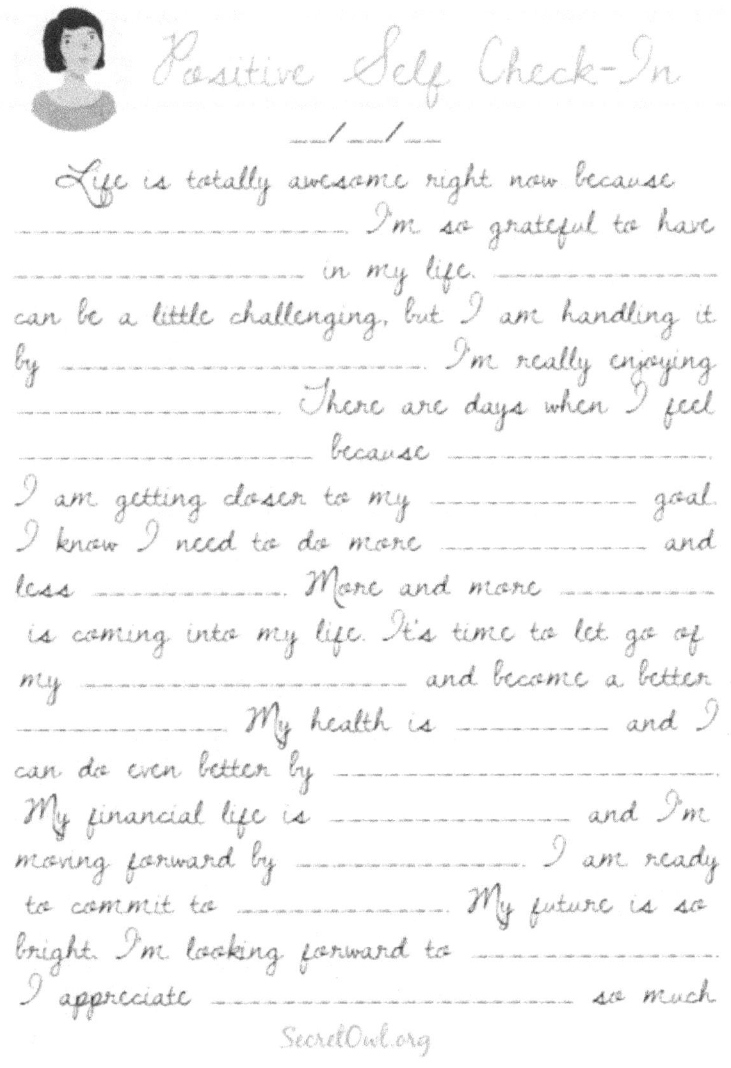

Positive Self Check-In

___/___/___

Life is totally awesome right now because
_____ I'm so grateful to have
_____ in my life. _____
can be a little challenging, but I am handling it
by _____ I'm really enjoying
_____ There are days when I feel
_____ because _____
I am getting closer to my _____ goal.
I know I need to do more _____ and
less _____ More and more _____
is coming into my life. It's time to let go of
my _____ and become a better
_____ My health is _____ and I
can do even better by _____
My financial life is _____ and I'm
moving forward by _____ I am ready
to commit to _____ My future is so
bright. I'm looking forward to _____
I appreciate _____ so much

SecretOwl.org

Figure 5.4 Secret Owl Positive Check-In
by Michelle Rohr of secretowl.org

the activities I have tried, this is one of my favorites. It really got me thinking about choosing which activity was most important and then how to represent it. (See Figure 5.5.) While this may not be something done daily or even weekly, I will use this idea for breaks (e.g., holiday breaks, spring break, summer) so I can track and record my time. It is also a fantastic activity to be used as a springboard for reflective writing after the break.

Figure 5.5: Doodle a Day for summer break

5.1f Explore Lists

You should check out the writing and drawing prompt books from the San Francisco Writers' Grotto. They recently published the book *642 Lists to Write*[5], and I jumped on it because I love lists. Lists are also much easier to conjure than a paragraph or poem, so they end up being less daunting to students. I mean, who wouldn't want to write about "Nine Things That Are Seriously Overrated" or "Three Possible Titles for Your Autobiography." There are also some especially clever ones listed like "Someone's Installed a Vending Machine Right outside Your Door. It's Personalized for You. What's in It?" I share these because documenting what we care about helps us better understand ourselves, and it allows us to see trends. What does that list of the last five songs I listened to or the last seven books I read tell me about myself, and/or what is going on with me right now? If you are planning to have students write a personal narrative at some point, these types of activities provide excellent fodder to blaze right through this process.

5.1g Explore Sentence Stems from Books

I realize this last idea is a bit of a stretch . . . at least in how I acquired the prompts. Know that this idea has percolated for a while, and I think it ties in nicely with the next chapter which covers what I do with the books I read. And one of those things is to keep a lexicon library. As I read fiction and/or nonfiction, there are certain sentences or words that jump out at me. Sometimes it is the cleverness in the way the words are structured. Sometimes it is a feeling the sentence evokes. Either way, I pick these like flowers to enjoy later. Below is one of my "bouquets":

- My wish for you is . . . (*How to Think Like Leonardo da Vinci* by Michael J. Gelb)

- I am from the school of thought that the . . . (*Long Story Short: The Only Storytelling Guide You'll Ever Need* by Margot Leitman)

- He found refuge in . . . (*Pivot: The Only Move That Matters Is Your Next One* by Jenny Blake)

- I reject the notion that . . . (*Shrill* by Lindy West)

- Make no mistake, there is a place for . . . (*The Coaching Habit: Say Less, Ask More, and Change the Way You Lead Forever* by Michael Bungay Stanier)

5.2 Reflections You Can Use (or Teach) to Explore Learning

Perhaps these reflective and journaling exercises were not your cup of tea. That's totally fine. Let's flip the coin a bit and focus on reflective activities that afford us the platform to explore ourselves as learners and professionals. The next five exercises, like the seven above, come from a variety of places. For these, I want to focus more on the types of activities and less about where you can uncover them (though I will share their origins).

5.2a *Student-Directed Queries*

Some teachers will argue that students are spoon-fed, that when you ask them to come up with an idea from scratch rather than complete a worksheet, they freeze. I argue that this is a learned skill that students need to practice. Students in our mentorship classes are required to spend two hours a week with a mentor in their field and must account for and reflect on those experiences. One of the ways students do that is by answering the weekly research question. One week's question might be "How does attitude come across in an email? When writing an email, how can attitude change the desired outcome of the message?" Eventually students must write their own research questions. One such student-generated question was "How does teamwork come into play when making diagnoses and providing recommendations for treatment to patients?" I share this idea because I think journaling and reflection, like all the other skills in these chapters, will start out as more prescriptive. At some point, though, we must loosen the reins and give students ownership over their own reflection—and even allow them to draft their own prompts.

5.2b Two Decision Models

The Decision Book is like the little black book to introspection. All fifty of the decision models are divided into four main categories:

- How to improve myself
- How to improve others
- How to understand myself better
- How to understand others better

It was difficult to share only two, but these are especially helpful for academic and professional use. One is the Rubber Band Model (Figure 5.6), which you can use for dealing with a dilemma or decision. Picture yourself being drawn in two directions, and ask yourself, What is holding me? and What is Pulling me?

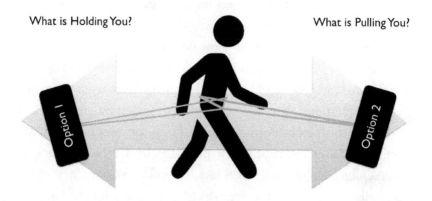

What is Holding You?

What is Pulling You?

Option 1

Option 2

Figure 5.6: Rubber Band Model adapted from
The Decision Book: 50 Models for Strategic Thinking
by Mikael Krogerus and Roman Tschappeler

The Making of Model (Figure 5.7) is another of my favorites. The original model was to be used to determine what is relevant from our past, what can be forgotten, and what we need to take with us. I adapted this one for academic use. What I love about it is how easily it could be used to reflect on a project, a class, a semester, a long-term goal, etc. Rather than assign meaning to an event in our past, I use it as a reflection cocktail with a garnish of gratitude. I look at the goal, what I learned (from the project, that class, etc.), any failures or mistakes I made and how I addressed them, successes along the way, and finally the people and how they helped me along the way. That might be my partner, a teacher, a librarian, etc. Too often we finish a class or a project, and we just move on to the next without properly reflecting on all the interworking parts that got us to the finish line.

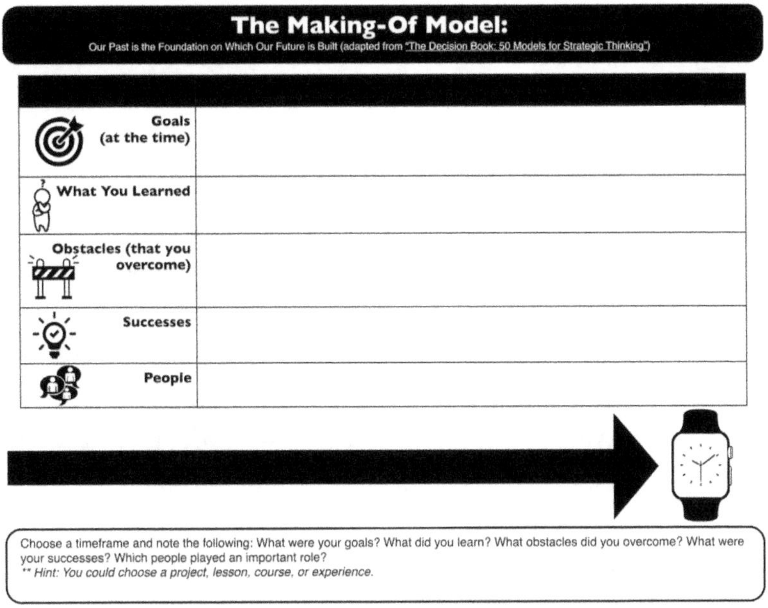

The Making-Of Model:
Our Past is the Foundation on Which Our Future is Built (adapted from "The Decision Book: 50 Models for Strategic Thinking")

🎯	**Goals (at the time)**	
	What You Learned	
	Obstacles (that you overcome)	
💡	**Successes**	
	People	

Choose a timeframe and note the following: What were your goals? What did you learn? What obstacles did you overcome? What were your successes? Which people played an important role?
** Hint: You could choose a project, lesson, course, or experience.

Figure 5.7: The Making of Model[6] adapted from *The Decision Book: 50 Models for Strategic Thinking* by Mikael Krogerus and Roman Tschappeler using Pages and Noun Project

5.2c Three Pathways for Life

This idea spawned from Stanford, which offers a course called "Designing Your Life" to Juniors and Seniors. I experienced a few of the activities offered throughout the course at a SXSWEDU workshop, where the trainers spoke about people's Odyssey years and the fact that many people are experiencing encore careers (a second and a third career). They spoke of dysfunctional beliefs like how students should already know what they want to be or where they are going by now. Their point was that there are multiple versions of you, and you must figure out which prototype fits the best. In this exercise (Figure 5.8), you draft out three five-year timelines in one-year increments. The first timeline is pretty much your current path. The second is your plan B (what you would be doing if you weren't doing what you are right now). And the last is what you would do if you didn't care about what people thought and money was no option.

Designing three pathways is not a novel concept, but you then add a dashboard that takes things to a new level. The dashboard includes four gauges: Resources, Likability, Confidence, and Coherence and a scale from zero to one hundred. You have three pathways, but on a scale of zero to one hundred, how much time, money, and skill do you have to make each of the three pathways a reality? How much do you like each plan? How confident are you in your ability to make each plan happen? And how does this plan align with your life? Not gonna lie, I love a good template, and this one did not disappoint.

5.2d Four Buckets for Work

Pivot: The Only Move that Matters is Your Next One by Jenny Blake is designed for the professional world, but its message is applicable to our students as well, especially to the CTE (Career and Technology Education) courses. I work very closely with our mentorship teacher. The mentorship class is one of my favorites, as it provides so much real-world exposure. Students really get a sense of what a job and career is from observing those in the field twice a week and reflecting on those observations. One of the tasks for the mentorship class is to design a resume. I come in and help with this process because visual literacy is so imperative. In Blake's book, the section on work buckets particularly struck my fancy and has been of great help as we address this project. She talks about four buckets or zones for the work we do. One side of the spectrum is "The Zone of Incompetence" and "The Zone of Competence." The first includes tasks at which we do not excel, and the second is tasks at which we might be competent, but others could perform as easily. On the other side of the spectrum

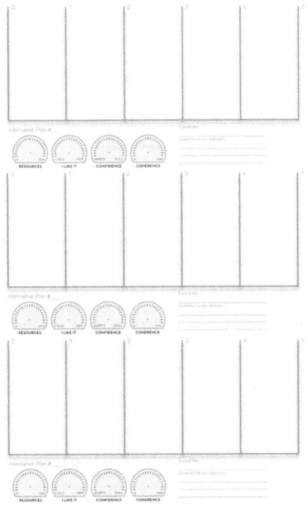

Figure 5.8: 3 Pathways to Design Your Life Copyright Evans Burnett LLC

are "The Zone of Excellence" and "The Zone of Genius." The first is activities we do very well, and the other is activities to which we are uniquely suited that call into play our individual gifts and strengths.

Why is this type of reflection important? First, if we are listing skills and tasks on a resume that we can do but perhaps don't enjoy doing rather than tasks and activities that we do exceedingly well and truly enjoy doing, we are setting ourselves up for failure. I encourage students to build a resume for the job you want, a job that suits you— not just a job.

5.2e Five-Star Learning Environment

This idea came to me while sitting in a PD session with instrumental jazz playing quietly. The intent of the music was to be calming while we worked, but I found it anything but. It was the type of music that I find distracting and even irksome. I love music, but my music has a slightly different flair, and what I listen to depends on the task at hand. If I am doing tasks like checking email or designing a flier, I can chill to my playlist with a little Macklemore, Twenty One Pilots, Blue October, etc. But if I need more focus, I might actually loop one song and play it over and over. That day I became so fascinated with music and mood that I created a Pinterest board to curate several articles and bits of research: pinterest.com/techchef4u/music-mood-and-learning.

For my youngest son, it isn't music that brings focus, but chewing gum. He seems to focus better, especially on cognitively taxing tasks, if he chews gum. I know music and gum might seem trivial in the grand scheme of things, but think about all the businesses that cater to these ideas and preferences. I am not saying we need to indulge every student's idiosyncratic preferences or to provide free snacks and napping tanks to our students, but I am suggesting that we allow our students to explore and advocate for working environments that they feel most productive both in and out of school. Some of the questions that are included in chapter two with the calendar template provide a nice framework for this topic.

To get to the heart of what environments work best for students engaging in both individual and group work, I tapped into the book *Caffeine for the Creative Team* and concocted an adaptation of their "I Got Smell" activity: I have students think about a time when they worked with other students and had a positive and successful experience. Have them consider all five of their senses. What music was playing? What did the space look like? What did it smell like? Where were they seated and in what type of chair? Did they have any food and beverages around? Students can craft their individual story and then share commonalities and differences or generate the story as a group. Once completed, the group can determine which sensory experiences are nice to have, which ones are must haves, and what elements are easy to provide (e.g., gum, water, a particular type of lighting and/or seating arrangement).

If you want to explore this project as a creative writing experiment, students could create their own ad for a work space. Have students write a real estate listing for their ideal or current work space. If they have no current work space, they could nab a picture of their nook of the library or take a picture of their desk or dining room table at home and bring it into school the next day. If creating an ideal space, they could search "Twenty-first-century learning spaces" or "creative work spaces" for inspiration. The activity is ultimately geared to have students identify environments in which they work best. Having students delve into this self-awareness and eventually share with a partner validates their own preferences while providing perspective into another's. Exploring the wording used on popular real estate fliers or even Craigslist ads will help students get familiarized with the type of common verbiage needed (e.g., "Complete with ____," "When you enter the ____," "Situated in the ____," "Enjoy the ____," Nestled in ____," "Perfectly suited for ____").

I remember sitting on the swing in Clarksville, Texas, with my dad at night listening to the whip-poor-wills and bobwhites. As I was the oldest, he would let me stay up a little later than my brothers and sit out on the porch swing. I would ask questions, and he would answer them. To this day, I have not lost that curiosity. Sure, I can now just do a Google deep dive or Ask Alexa to determine the radius of the earth, but there are things that even my father, Google, and Alexa can't answer. These are things to which only I know the answer. I couldn't very well title this chapter "A Long Conversation with a Talking Caterpillar," but the thought crossed my mind because this chapter is really about answering the question "Who are you?"

5.3 What Other Accoutrements Can Accompany a Journal?

We have covered both personal and professional journaling prompts. But as with any of the chapter topics, everything is malleable. I really want you to make it your own, so I thought I should share more on how I do that as well. Below are several examples of additional things I add to my journal, broken down into three categories:

5.3a Audits

The first thing I do when I start a new journal is conduct an audit of the last one (Figure 5.9). What worked? What didn't? What lists will I use again? What organizational structure did I like? What will I do differently? These can be done from semester to semester or year to year. And they are simple. I just create a table and note things I liked about the last journal and things I didn't like or wanted to change. Another spin on this might be a Keep/Change/Delete table. This process allows you to reflect on your reflective practice and continue to fine-tune it.

Figure 5.9: My bullet journal audit, lists of what I LOVED and will do again—and what I LEARNED and will change featuring washi tape from James Burke @jameslukeburkecreative on Instagram

5.3b Lifestyle Lists

As you well know, I love lists. They are easy to generate, and they are fantastic snapshots of a moment in time. I make lists of places I want to go, current music in my playlist, Netflix shows I am watching, favorite camera apps, restaurants where I want to eat, my favorite sites for ephemera (vintage pictures and memorabilia). Blue October has a song titled "The Worry List," so I also keep a worry list of all the things that are bothering me. It could be a relationship. It could be a concern with my boys. Just writing it down and acknowledging it lets me breathe a bit more easily. And as we are poor historians of our feelings, keeping the worry list helps me put things into perspective and know that these problems are fleeting. If the problem is still there in a few weeks or months, I then know that it is a bigger concern and requires another strategy to tackle it.

5.3c Graphs, Mind Maps, and Tables

I include several of these within my journal. If I take an online quiz and it spits out a graph, I will copy it and include it within my journal with my thoughts on the results. I also do this with the results of personality or professional surveys like StrengthsFinder. Figure 5.10 depicts the results of the Introversion Traits quiz via nymag.com that breaks down four types of introversion and provides you more context as to what each means. If you plan on doing one of these personally or with your students, I highly advise using the personality test via 16personalities.com.

Sometimes something tickles my fancy, and I decide to go off the beaten trail. This happened while I was watching *Ozark* on Netflix. Each episode starts with an O and four icons within it. At first you don't pay much attention to them, but soon you realize that each one of the icons are keys to unlocking the secrets of that episode, so I played with that idea for my own journal with personal observations (Figure 5.11).

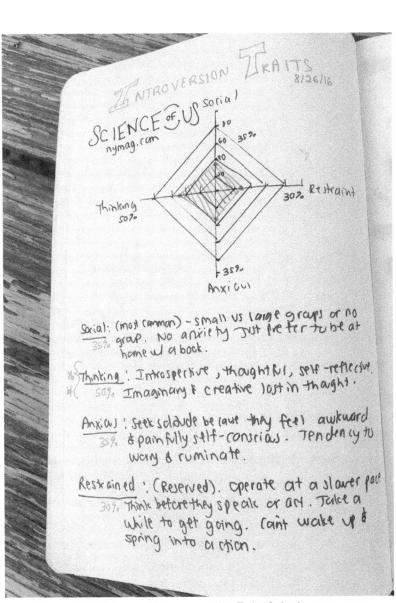

Figure 5.10: "Science of Us" Introversion Traits Quiz via *nymag.com*

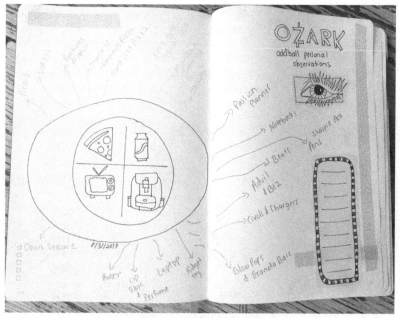

Figure 5.11: *Ozark*-themed Mind Map featuring stickers
from Dylusions Dyan Reavelely

One of my favorite reflection activities thus far has been a photo reflection. I built a table comprised of twelve cells (Figure 5.12). Then I sort through my phone's gallery in the monthly album view. While this doesn't let me see everything I did that month, it gives me a good idea of memorable events, which I jot down in the corresponding month cell. I also consult my Google Calendar and/or planner for any other events or moments I might have missed. One could do a similar activity by scanning through a social media feed. This activity could also double as a gratitude list because it forces you to realize that even though you may not have achieved every goal you set out to achieve, there is much for which to be grateful.

I don't want you to trip over your own two feet looking over your shoulder or in the rear-view mirror, but I do think when we

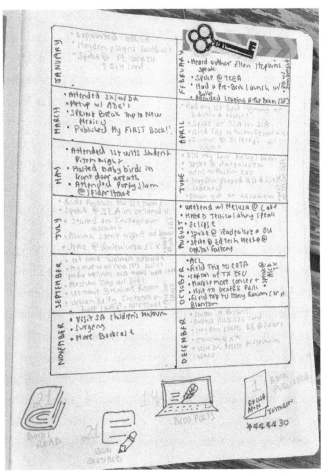

Figure 5.12: Yearly gratitude and productivity audit

change lanes or set a new course, we should be cognizant of what lies behind and around us. And these activities encompassed here allow us to move safely forward by acknowledging the moments and events that surround us as we build or constantly hone our own identity. You might have seen Heidi Swapp products at Michael's. She is a big believer in storytelling and scrapbooking. During her keynote at Wild for Planners (I attended a planner conference, and it was every bit as amazing as I had hoped it would be), she notes that the way she stops the blur (e.g., "today was just a blur") is to honor herself and write down things. It kind of reminds me of the movie *Click* in which Adam Sandler is given a magic remote. It starts picking up on his habits. As he begins fast-forwarding through moments, the device learns these preferences and automatically fast-forwards through his life until years become a blur. While this movie is clearly fiction, I think there is a point to be made. The cure for the blur is journaling and reflection, and while we (us and our students) certainly don't need to do this daily (although you could), once a week or every six weeks would definitely clear a bit of the fog.

In his book, *Along Came a Leader: A Guide to Personal and Professional Leadership*, Kelly Croy notes, "The ingredients we mix into a bowl determine the dish we prepare."[7] Half the battle is taking note of the ingredients, and the other half of the battle is deciding what they mean. And we can't do either unless we take time to slow down the blur. One more food metaphor comes to mind, this one from Rod Judkins and *The Art of Creative Thinking*. Judkins states, "You can borrow flour, but you have to make your own bread."[8] I sincerely hope you and your students borrow from these ideas and then do the deep work necessary to let the metaphorical bread rise to the occasion.

AWESOME AMULET CHECKLIST

☐ My students understand and can articulate the benefits of journaling and self-reflection.

☐ My students engage with a variety of personal reflection prompts (e.g., lists, fill in the blanks, letters, poems, drawings, etc.).

☐ My students use apps that track data in conjunction with self-reflection.

☐ My students express gratitude to their peers, teachers, family, and beyond.

☐ My students have the opportunity to discuss their reflections with others.

☐ My students can write, research, and answer their own reflection questions.

☐ My students can make decisions based on a variety of models (e.g., dashboard, buckets, etc.).

☐ My students are aware of how their environment impacts their learning and can articulate and advocate for these elements.

☐ My students have strategies for completing a journal audit from semester to semester or year to year.

☐ My students add other visuals to the journals and reflections like mind-maps and graphs.

☐ My students have internalized journaling and reflection.

WAKEFUL WHIMSY CORE IDEAS

- **English Language Arts:** Have students research famous people that kept journals or diaries. A few to start with could be Albert Einstein, Frida Kahlo, and Queen Victoria. Have them note the trends and styles and make a list of three to five things they would like to try. A more modern take would be to have them follow #journal or #journaling on Instagram and find three people that share their ideas or journals, again noting and listing the same things.

- **Math and Science:** Choose a famous mathematician and/or scientist. Research how they reflect on failure, mathematical theorems, and the scientific process. Choose one mathematician and/or scientist and complete one of the reflective journaling activities as if you were that individual.

- **Social Studies:** Have students design a journal for a historical, fictional, or literary figure. What features will it have? What will it look like? What writing prompts and lists would it include? Explain/Justify.

SHARE YOUR OWN EXAMPLES AND IDEAS INSPIRED BY THIS CHAPTER. BE SURE TO TAG YOUR COMMENTS: #CREATIVELYPRODUCTIVE.

Citations

1. Smit, Irene & Hulst, Astrid van der. 2017. A book that takes its time: An Unhurried Adventure in Creative Mindfulness (Flow). Workman Publishing Company.

2. Platform.Potter Gift. Q and a a Day. Potter Style. 2010.

3. Trinidad, Angela Passion Planner. Passion Planner LLC. 2018.

4. Toepfer, Steven M.; Cichy, Kelly & Peters, Patti. 2011. "Letters of Gratitude: Further Evidence for Author Benefits." Journal of Happiness Studies 13 (1): 187-201. Springer Nature. doi:10.1007/s10902-011-9257-7.

5. San Francisco Writers' Grotto. 642 Lists to Write. Chronicle Books Llc. 2017.

6. Krogerus, Mikael; Tschäppeler, Roman & Piening, Jenny. 2012. The decision book. New York: W.W. Norton & Co.

7. Croy, Kelly. 2015. Along Came a Leader: A Guide to Personal and Professional Leadership. CreateSpace Independent Publishing.

8. Judkins, Rod. 2016. The art of creative thinking. TarcherPerigee.

Research

- Achor, Shawn. 2011. "Transcript of "The happy secret to better work"." Ted.com. ted.com/talks shawn_achor_the_happy_secret_to_better_work/transcript?language=en.

- Baker, Ashley. "Mentorship Questions." Mentorship class at Westlake High School, 2018.

- Blake, Jenny. 2017. Pivot. Portfolio.

- Cometry. 2018. "Educational Programs." COMETRY. cometry.org/educational-programs.html.

- Han, Jenny. 2014. To all the boys I've loved before. (To all the boys I've loved before (Series), #1.). New York: SSBFYR.

- Harms, William. 2011. "Writing about worries eases anxiety and improves test performance." University of Chicago News. news.uchicago.edu/story/writing-about-worries-eases-anxiety-and-improves-test-performance.

- Lewis, Tanya L., "Facebook Emotions Are Contagious," *Scientific American*, scientificamerican.com/article/facebook-emotions-are-contagious/. 2014.

- Mumaw, Stefan & Oldfield, Wendy. 2009. Caffeine for the creative team. Cincinnati, Ohio: HOW Books.

- Pennebaker, James W. 2013. The secret life of pronouns. New York: Bloomsbury Press.

- Pennebaker, James W & Evans, John F. 2014. Expressive writing. Enumclaw, WA: Idyll Arbor.

- Wiley-Blackwell. "It's the little things: Everyday gratitude as a booster shot for romantic relationships." ScienceDaily. sciencedaily.com/releases/2010/05/100524072912.htm (accessed October 22, 2018).

- Zomorodi, Manoush. 2017. Bored and brilliant. St. Martin's Press.

CHAPTER 6

Read, Write, Review

That's a great deal to make one word mean.
—Alice, Through the Looking-Glass

When I make a word do a lot of
work like that, I always pay it extra.
—Humpty Dumpty, Through the Looking-Glass

Amulet: Book

In a chapter focused on reader's and writer's notebooks, I feel I would be leading you astray or at the very least not painting the full picture if I didn't start with some words devoted to reading. I realize this chapter's topic is the biggest stretch of all the chapters. People are hard-pressed to deny the need for students to develop the skills of time management, organization, goal-setting, and reflection, but reading and note-taking do not top the list in some educators' books. Reading and writing are taught in school, but they almost always become part of the surroundings, and we forget to explain how these skills should evolve and be used in the future. While each of the next four paragraphs may seem disjointed, they all inform our current landscape of education and literacy. Stay with me.

In an article by *The Globe and Mail* titled, "I have forgotten how to read,"[1] Michael Harris notes, "Our sense of time has always been warped by our technologies. Church bells segmented the day into intervals. Factory whistles ushered workers. But the current barrage of alerts and pings leaves us more warped than ever."[1] His goal and message is to read more deeply and without interruptions.

Patrick Sullivan is an English professor at Manchester Community College and the author of *A New Writing Classroom, Listening, Motivation, and Habits of Mind*. Something he said in an open letter on aaup.org (American Association of University Professors) piqued my interest. He mentioned a study by Alice Sullivan that showed reading for pleasure produces important benefits across a variety of academic disciplines (including math) and that "reading is actually linked to increased cognitive process over time."[2] There were other studies which noted "the influence of language skills developed through reading, conversation, and family life 'never ceases to be felt' across an individual's life."[2] Mr. Sullivan was not referring to surface reading, but to deeper reading, which requires "intellectual generosity."[2]. This type of reading encompasses not only memorization and recall but reflection and sustained concentration. His message is that we should enjoy reading and read without distraction.

An article from *Time* noted a study finding "individuals who often read fiction appear to be better able to understand other people, empathize with them and view the world from their perspective."[3] Another study from the same article stated that students who read exclusively "onscreen were three times less likely to say they enjoy reading very much and a third less likely to have a favorite book"[3]and "two times less likely to be above-average readers than those who read daily in print or both in print and onscreen."[3] Their message is to show students how to read deeply rather than superficially like many do on the web.

If you are a math or science teacher, please don't tune me out. With secondary students, I have used a variety of children's books ranging from *What's Your Angle, Pythagoras?* (not to be confused with R.E.M.'s "What's the Frequency, Kenneth?") and *The Greedy Triangle* to *The Sir Cumference* series. Just recently I serendipitously happened upon the *Mindshift* article "How Reading Novels in Math Class Can Strengthen Student Engagement," which highlighted how both a seventh-grade pre-algebra teacher (Joel Bezaire) and a twelfth-grade calculus teacher (Sam Shah) use novels like *The Curious Incident of the Dog in the Night Time* and *Flatland*. One quote from the *Mindshift* article especially resonated with me: "Students who more easily self-identify as 'English types' immediately get a little more comfortable in math class if they experience those types of (literary) questions regularly."[4] Too often we think about reading in English and social studies but forget that each discipline has a literacy and that we can read and write in every content area. What I love about this idea is the "surprisingly educational" nature of these books. Their message is to use literature to humanize mathematics and to jumpstart curiosity.

There are also studies that state "engaged reading can overcome traditional barriers to reading achievement, including gender, parental education, and income."[5]. And according to the Organization for Economic Co-operation and Development, reading for pleasure was found to be "the most important indicator of the future success of the child."[6]

So what are you getting at exactly, Lisa? Here are three takeaways:

1. Learners should experience and engage with a balance of both digital and analog reading.

2. Learners of all ages should read outside their edusphere or content sphere if they want to ignite creativity and curiosity.

3. Learners of all ages should have a choice in what they read to acquire an intrinsic desire for reading and thirst for knowledge and stories.

6.1 Why Should I Read Books from outside the Edusphere?

Back in the academic school year of 2011–2012, a little over a year after the generation 1 iPad was released, I began cohosting a podcast series on iTunes titled *Appy Hours 4 U*. Every four or five episodes, we would share a Surprisingly Educational-themed episode, and they were always the most popular of the lot. We shared how people could use apps like Talking Tom for math word problems, Aroundertouch and Epic Citadel for creative writing, and Typedrawing for practicing foreign languages. These podcasts spurred sessions, workshops, and webinars on surprisingly educational uses of edutainment apps which were always highly attended for two reasons: (1) People like learning about engaging ways to use technology, and (2) people are always interested in how others generate creative and sometimes unexpected ideas to impact existing curriculum.

Recently, our school hosted a student-led staff PD session during which a student highlighted all the features of the Notability app that she uses. At the very end, she mentioned that there are also creative unintended uses of apps; for example, while Notability is not designed to be a drawing app per se, the highlighter can create depth and layers. She opened up an image of a girl's braided pony tail that was beautifully drawn and zoomed in to show how it was just layers of highlighting. In Ryan Holiday's book *Perennial Seller*, he mentioned that his books are typically written for people in the industry of sales, creating, and marketing. Interestingly, an athlete picked up his book *The Obstacle is the Way*, and suddenly NFL athletes were a surprising and unexpected audience for his book on stoicism. I share all of this to spark the discussion on getting out of our silos. When we all review and share content created solely by educators and/or the educational realm or solely designed for our specific content area, we miss out on ideas and solutions that we may never have had and/or found if we hadn't stepped off the beaten path.

One of my most retweeted and shared blog posts was a book list with my personal notes and recommendations. The list highlights twenty industry books (books not explicitly designed for the edusphere) and then shares six more that are designed for the classroom. Because I think reading is so vital to both our personal and professional lives and those of our students, I wanted to share a few of these with you. Get ready to fill your Amazon cart or the satchel you take to the library with some surprisingly educational reads.

- **Steal Like an Artist and Show Your Work:** You cannot escape the reach these books have had. I see them mentioned in sessions for librarians and writer's workshops and have even found them translated in Spanish in a bookstore in Monterrey, Neuvo Leon, Mexico (Figure 6.1). If you are not familiar with Austin Kleon's books, you might know him for his epic blackout poetry. While his books are designed for both authors and creators, his ideas truly transcend all fields. *Steal Like an Artist* delves into how we should share online, the difference between good and bad theft when it comes to people's ideas and work, and the importance of fan letters and praise files. *Show Your Work* highlights the need for a scenius (essentially a global PLN) and stresses the importance of focusing on the process over the product and the ability to take a punch (e.g., handle criticism).

Figure 6.1: Me holding Austin Kleon's book *Show Your Work* in Monterrey Bookstore

- *The Secret Lives of Color:* This book looks at seventy-five different shades of color and discusses their historical, cultural, and literary origins and meanings as well as how they were made and which artists use them; for example, the pigment Prussian Blue was first used in blueprints, and green appears in the flags of predominantly Islamic countries because "paradise" is synonymous with "garden." Other facts I gleaned were the strict girl-pink and boy-blue dividing line only dates from the mid-20th century. And did you know that in Shakespeare's day, green costumes were considered bad luck on stage? Oh, and did you know French soldiers serving in Africa were given absinthe to ward off malaria? This book would be great as a companion for an Art History course or a way to enlighten or highlight a World History course or content that students are reading in an English class. It is also a stellar way to dip your toe into color psychology (mentioned later in this chapter).

- *A Book That Takes Its Time:* This book is an analog maker-space match made in heaven. Picture a magazine with lots of really well-written articles and illustrations paired with lots of analog goodies and activities like postcards to send to friends to show you care, notecards to document beautiful moments, and a mini thirty-day notebook on mindful analysis as well as stickers to share nostalgia. This book was a joy to read, view, and explore. (*Flow* magazine has a most amazing Instagram account as well.) Perfect for anyone looking to explore mindfulness and social emotional learning skills in the classroom, and yet I can tell you it will most likely not be on anyone's back-to-school reading list until now.

- *Flawd:* This one is perfect for a secondary student book study (again with the turquoise and teal covers). It tackles bullying from the perspective of a girl that was bullied, then became a bully, then overcame the hate. Picture a mash-up of Austin Kleon meets *A Book That Takes Its Time.* I loved every page; in fact, I even used her idea of the masks for an activity in the social media chapter of *Cultivating Communication in the Classroom.* The idea was that we all wear masks, and we play roles that people see, but we aren't our masks; we are the only ones that see behind the mask, and this is what we see of ourselves. If you are talking about digital citizenship with students, this book is a must!

- *No Good Card for This:* In an age where listening skills and oral and written communication are so vital, the idea of navigating circumstances with compassion and empathy are integral. And these ladies provide so many practical activities from figuring out what type of non-listener you are (e.g., the optimist, sage, doomsayer, or the epidemiologist) to strategies to create a gesture wall (e.g., ideas to help someone in need) or even incorporating better phrases (e.g., rather than "I felt _____ when I _____," one could say, "What's that like for you?").[7] Many of the ideas have made me a better leader, colleague, and collaborator, and I am ever so grateful for these two ladies.

- *The Decision Book:* This book (also mentioned in Chapter 5) would be a poor excuse for an audio book, as it basically details fifty graphics or models used by businesses to make a variety of decisions. It does have a paragraph or so that details how the model should be used and what its origins are. I must tell you that I have used many of these tools with students in career and tech classes as well as reflections for reader's and writer's notebooks. I even used one of the models, the Uffe Elbaek, in the collaboration chapter of *Cultivating Communication in the Classroom.* Like a quick Myer's Briggs test, it is such a great way to get a feel for a student's strengths and weaknesses and/ or preferences.

- **Crank:** The only fiction book in the batch, *Crank* is riveting, and many of our secondary students have read it. When we teach poetry, we don't always look to current authors for inspiration. True, the topics of Ellen Hopkin's books are dark. The *Crank* series is loosely based on her daughter's addiction to meth. But it is her expert use of alliteration, anaphora, concrete poems, and wordsmithing that left me hankering for more.

I have a bit of serendipity with books. I wouldn't quite say it is cosmic and/or religious per se, but I think everyone stumbles upon answers to life's deepest questions in their own way. For me, it has always been with books. Sometimes it is movies too. Sometimes I find what I am looking for and sometimes I uncover the answer to something I didn't even realize was a question. Either way, there is a power to persistently digging deeper through thoughts and ideas that aren't impeded by pop-ups or an online word count. Don't get me wrong. I think blogs and web articles have their place, and I learn a lot from both. But if that is the only type of media we and/or our students are consuming, I think we are missing out on a magical untapped world.

I share these books because they have been invaluable to my practice and to the content I create and share with students and educators alike. But this chapter isn't really about reading; it is about what we do with what we read and consume as learners. So now that you have a new box of books arriving on your doorstep in forty-eight hours or less—or instantly to your e-reader—perhaps you will join me on a ride.

6.2 How Do We Retain What We Read?

Reading and writing tend to work harmoniously. Which is why it is surprising that we don't naturally spend more time modeling and sharing the process of using writer's and reader's notebooks with our students. The writer's and reader's notebook is not a new concept, but I will venture to say that this tool is underutilized or often contrived. I started keeping a reader's and a writer's notebook three years ago and have found it instrumental in my ability to write my first book and this one. I would also argue that it is foundational to my deeper knowledge of the content I read and how I apply it to my work and my daily life, both personally and professionally. With that said, I would like to dive into the path that led me to this practice and then share my process.

I have always been a bibliophile and very much a word nerd. I kept both a journal and a scrapbook all throughout most of my academic career. When I was in high school, I read novels and textbooks. Most of those novels were fiction, and I am ashamed to admit a few V.C. Andrews books might have been added to the lot as well. When I was in college and completing my master's degree, I read novels, textbooks, online research, and journals.

When I started working professionally as an educator, I added professional and industry books to the list. These books were, dare I say, of my choosing and supported my field that I found surprisingly educational, although they weren't books I picked up for a class. I relished highlighting them and then promptly set them back on my shelf. And there was something of a letdown. I read it, and I felt energized, but that energy and insight seemed to have an expiration date: my memory—and the older I get, the more it seems to fade. (Although for some odd reason I can still recite the prologue to Romeo and Juliet, which I memorized my freshman year in high school. Go figure.) To regain some of that energy, I started revisiting these books and jotting down their gems within my notebook (call it an adult dialectical diary if you will). The active process of writing down these notes as well as reviewing and transcribing the content I had read seemed to revitalize it for me. I seriously felt like a genius in meetings when I could mention a quote or a research study by simply flipping through my notebook. And I found the notebook itself started to take on a life of its own. Now no one is getting sucked into the notebook like Jumanji or anything, but I can say that I wanted to read more and found that what I was reading was retained. I was also able to make more connections across multiple works simply because my thoughts and insights were distilled into one place—and I returned to this place often.

I draw from much of my reader's notebook when I write, and I hope your students will too. Sometimes we must set something down and come back to it for it to really bloom in our understanding. I wish I had the ability to write this book in one sitting or even a month, but it took many months of drafting ideas, letting them lie dormant, then returning to them, nurturing them, and letting them grow.

As it turns out, Ryan Holiday, Austin Kleon, and I share a similar system for reading and note-taking. But Austin and Ryan take it one step further. While I read and take notes in my books and then transfer said notes to my journal, Austin and Ryan use a middle man: the index card. They transfer their notes to note cards and then go back through the notecards for themes, then assemble their ideas. Austin notes, "There's a kind of constant creative revisiting that goes on, one that leads to new ideas, and new writing. (Re-vision is re-*seeing*.)"[8] It's not so peculiar. The idea of waiting and reseeing allows us to see there might "be something there that wasn't there before." You don't even have to live in an enchanted castle with a talking candlestick to discover it.

Before we dive headfirst into the world of reader's notebooks, I would like to share a disclaimer. Please know that I am not one for fads. I do mention nostalgia and trends in the introduction to anchor my ideas and process to alleviate your conclusions that I may be a fly-by-night #scrapnotes shaman. Those who know me from my blog, my book *Cultivating Communication in the Classroom,* and my social media presence, know that I am one that shares vetted ideas, tools, and processes that work for me and the students and staff I support in hopes that they may fill a need for you too. As with all the other tools I've shared in this book, I promise to only share things that I love and use and/or have tried. I like to give you options so you can choose the fit that's right for you.

I am not one to create social media accounts unless I have a purpose for them, so I was a bit of a latecomer to Instagram; in fact, I didn't create the account till the summer of 2017. I had been doing this art journaling, scrap notes, book summary thing, and I wanted to have a venue to share some of the examples and connect with others that were doing the same thing, so I created "NoteChef4u" on Instagram (Figure 6.2), a sister of "TechChef4u." And while I do share my notes for others, the irony is not lost on me that there is decidedly and intentionally a lack of technology shared on that site. The digital world is here to stay, but I think we must strike a healthy balance.

Call me crazy, but I don't read e-books. I like the feeling and experience of a tangible book, and I like seeing the books on a shelf. But I do like to post online and blog about what I read, and sometimes I think in tweets and Facebook post paragraphs. Realizing that got me to thinking: *How much of my waking hours and thoughts are thinking about and composing writing and content for others, and how much time is spent on writing for myself?* Make no mistake, I love blogging, writing, and sharing on social media, but I had to wonder about the value of letting ideas germinate and flourish before sharing. When do I ruminate and extend my own thinking before clicking the "post" button? This pondering combined with my need to retain and utilize the content I read led me to create my own reader's notebook. Please don't put blinders on if you are not an avid reader; you could very well

notechef4u   Edit Profile   ⚙

544 posts   574 followers   536 following

Lisa Johnson Author of "Cultivating Communication in the Classroom" | 📱 📚,| 📱 taking 📷,| 📱 taking 📷 on what I read in 📚! I have a pension for art, analog, & teal.
www.techchef4u.com

———
POSTS   SAVED

Figure 6.2: NoteChef4u on Instagram

use the strategies I share next with TED Talks you watch, articles you read, or even podcasts to which you have listened. I incorporate all these things into my journal as well.

6.3 The Process for Summarizing a Book or Other Piece of Media

I enjoy reading, both personally and professionally, and I am one of those people who loves to highlight my books. Over time I built up a library of books with highlights and Post-its but no easy way to commit that info to memory or practice, or to easy access—until now. I call this process scrapnotes or scrap-noting. As the name suggests, it is a process of scrapbooking and note-taking during which I highlight or note scraps or pieces of the book that are specifically important to me. I should also mention that while I am talking analog note-taking with washi and pens, all of this can be done on an iPad and/or computer with font colors and shapes or even a dash of Canva and a dollop of Noun Project. So without further ado, here is my process:

Summarizing can seem like a trivial skill in the grand scheme of things, but it is essential if we want to internalize and utilize the content we consume. Though I encourage you to eventually create your own process, it is oftentimes useful to try a process that works for others as a model, then tweak as you go. So I am sharing a six-part process I have crafted and evolved over the past few years.

Before I do that, I wanted to share a "nice to have." This isn't necessarily a definitive part of the process, but it is helpful. Oftentimes when we have students create a writer's and/or reader's notebook, we have them decorate the cover with things they like or pictures of themselves. Something I started about four notebooks back was finding a sticker that embodied a mood, goal, an ethereal focus, or term I really enjoyed (e.g., joy, passion, whimsy). Because one of my first notebooks started with a unicorn sticker, I wanted to continue the trend with magical creatures, so the next notebook had a mermaid. As it turns out there are only so many mythological creatures for which one can easily find stickers. Centaurs and cyclops aren't that easy to find, and they don't make for a very welcoming entrance to my notebook either; thus, I changed my theme a bit. This next notebook has a sticker of Frida Kahlo. Austin Kleon does something similar. He chooses a patron saint or guardian spirit for his journals. Two of his most recent were Emily Dickinson and Tove Jansson. This selection could guide the types of books and content you select to read (e.g. a mythical creature like a unicorn denotes whimsy, purity, or wonder). It also helps easily decipher which journal is which.

Read and highlight.

Step one is reading and highlighting the book. If it is a book I own, I highlight in it. If I don't own it, I strategically place post-it notes so I remember the passage to which I want to return. With a podcast and/or TED Talk, I would listen to it and pause as things resonated with me and take note of those in my notebook.

Tuck away.

After I read the book, I always set the book down for a few weeks. This allows me to revisit the book with fresh eyes when I go back and review the highlights. I tend to make better decisions about what highlights were really important and then I only transcribe and scrapnote those.

Concoct a visual theme.

I create a page for the book that includes the title, author, and the date on which I am transcribing the notes. I also like to mimic the font and color of the book. Sometimes I play with color psychology and mood. If this idea appeals to you, you can take a Google deep

Figure 6.3: Visual themes in reader's notebook from *Crank*
by Ellen Hopkins[9] using washi tape by Molshine

dive through "color psychology" and/or check out one of my Pinterest
boards where I have curated over two hundred resources. For Ellen
Hopkins's book *Crank*, it has beautiful poetry, but the story is dark, so
I used green and black pens and washi tape that had a mystic, almost
gothic, quality to it (Figure 6.3).

For *Alice in Wonderland*, I used pink, black, and lots of ephemera (e.g., objects that are essentially old, like antique papers or library
cards) to set the mood. For *A Book That Takes Its Time*, I incorporated
pinks, reds, and peaches and included images of flowers and birds to
mirror the overall mood and tone of the book which is happy, calm,
and uplifting (Figure 6.4).

For Emily Dickinson's *Envelope Poems*, I used a smattering of
ephemera and added an envelope with a library card that included

Figure 6.4: Visual themes in reader's notebook from
A Book That Takes Its Time[10]

Figure 6.5: Visual themes in reader's notebook from Emily Dickinson's
Envelope Poems[11] using Jane Davenport confetissue pieces
(transparent stickers) and washi tape by Molshine

one of my favorite poems from the book. I also added washi tape that looked like old envelopes and pieces of another roll that had a Gothic Venus antique vibe (Figure 6.5).

When I did a sketch summary of *There Is No Good Card for This* (a book that is a social and emotional journey through gracefully handling difficult conversations and events), I took into account the mood and the message and used blue because it signifies trust and loyalty and green because it is both soothing and peaceful and signifies growth.

Ultimately I try to use different color palettes and pairings for each book I summarize so that way all the pages that pertain to that book look the same, but the entire notebook doesn't look the same. This strategy makes it easier to locate a book's section simply by flipping through the journal. I should also mention that I add all the notes in chronological order, each book summary one after the other. If you feel like this is too fanciful, I should mention that this is really what an illustrator gets paid to do. And in many of the books I read, there are no pictures and/or illustrations, so I feel like sometimes I need to add the visual meaning for myself. The process is less about adding imagery to notes as it is about finding and assigning meaning to what we read.

Create a color hierarchy.

Once I choose a color scheme that fits with the mood/tone of the book I am summarizing, I assign one of the colors as the lead color (e.g., to be used for headers) and the other as the subordinate color (e.g., for sub headers or basic text). When I was working on adding notes from Ellen Hopkins's books, I used black to write most of the poems, as the story is dark. Then I essentially wrote other parts of the poem or words I wanted to highlight using green (Figure 6.3). She does wonders with prose and dialogue, alliteration, and anaphora, and using two colors brought this idea to life. This practice also provides a clean visual hierarchy and some order to the anarchy of a blank page.

Visualize with icons.

We live in a world that is increasingly visual in nature. Icons tend to encompass a multitude of ideas and are easily recognizable. While I can't conjure and draw these visuals from memory like a proper scrapnotes shaman should, I am able to look at icon sites and recreate similar visuals. This very practice of assigning a visual to an idea or word has made me far more attune with metaphors, visual equations, and this practice. Figure 6.6 depicts an example of some of the notes I took while watching a TED Talk.

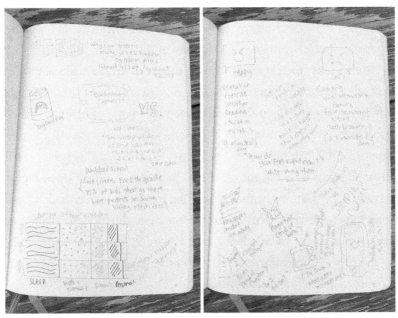

Figure 6.6: An example of a sketchnoted TED Talk.[12]

Embellish away.

Wait! Wait! You had me, Lisa, you really had me. And then you started adding in washi tape, and you lost me. Okay, bear with me here. Please know this is part evolution for me and part visual style preference. At first, my notes were mostly text in outline form. Then I started exploring icons and some sketchnoting practices. I then discovered washi tape, and it literally changed my world. I found that it was a nice way to break up text and add visual dividers or emphasize visual hierarchy. I couldn't tell you when in that process it turned into a wee bit of an addiction, but I will tell you that the washi tape, stickers, labels, and mementos became more for me than an embellishment. I wouldn't say that I am a sticker savant of sorts, but I have started becoming more strategic in the images and mementos I include. If I am using my Moleskine or Leuchtturm1917 (which I do for my book summaries), the pages tend to be a little thinner. This is when I take notecards, postcards, scraps of art, or really anything that adds to the content (both in idea or visually). I add these items in with permanent double-sided tape, then I get fanciful with my embellishments and add washi tape and stickers. You could totally leave the fanciful embellishments out, but I must tell you that this is one of my favorite parts; it's what makes me so happy each time I open a page to review my notes. Another thing I have noticed is that these visuals tend to heighten my memory for the book and the process. I can often remember where I was when I took the notes and what I was doing at the time. I can even visualize the entire page of notes, which I am unable to do with a basic outline.

I would like to get a bit more granular with this, as multiple people have asked me about the organization of this process. While I am transcribing notes, I typically keep a page for the following:

- **Research:** I am always collecting research, and I don't always want to return to the book to recall a percentage or study. Oftentimes I keep these research pages as a bulleted list. If the book is research-heavy, then I include two to three pages devoted just to this (Figure 6.7). If there isn't much research in the book and/or I would like to keep the research together with pertinent content in the chapter, I just weave it into pages chronologically with the quotes and the corresponding page numbers from the book.

Figure 6.7: Research gage gleaned from the book *The Coaching Habit: Say Less, Ask More, and Change the Way You Lead Forever*[13] by Michael Bungay Stanier with a Pete the Cat sticker

- **Lexicon Library:** Words and I have a bit of a chicken/egg relationship. Do I love words because I am an author? Or am I an author because I love words? I will most likely never make sense of that causality dilemma, but I can tell you that I have always had an affinity for words and phrases. Anything that tickles my fancy gets added here (Figure 6.8). As this is oftentimes not the main point of the book or my summarization, sometimes I will paste a card to a page so I can add this info there. This way it doesn't detract from the content I am summarizing. Official writer's notebook sites might refer to these phrases that we jot down as "mentor sentences," as they could be used as models for our own writing.

- **Quotes and Insight:** Obviously I don't write down every little thing from the book. Quotes to which I may want to refer back, ideas that have some merit or seem sticky, and processes I would like to try seem to get added the most. I should also mention that I include page numbers by all of these so I can easily return to the book and locate more info about them if the need arises.

The best advice I can impart to you is just start. My process has evolved and been honed and fine-tuned over the past two years (and really my lifetime). If I had waited for it to be perfect, I would never have discovered which way to go. Sometimes when you wander, you find your path. Truly this process is very personalized. Our district read *Switch* as a book study, and my colleague Debbie Smith and I both decided to take analog notes on the book. As you would imagine, our notes looked different (Figure 6.9a and b) and perhaps noted different scraps of the book yet were still an accurate summary of what we had read.

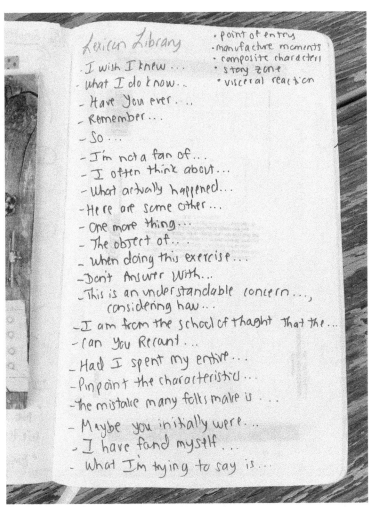

Figure 6.8: Lexicon library page gleaned from the book *Long Story Short: The Only Storytelling Guide You'll Ever Need*[14] by Margot Leitman

Figure 6.9a: Comparison of notes on book study of *Switch: How to Change Things when Change is Hard*[15] by Chip and Dan Heath. These notes from Debbie Smith.

Figure 6.9b: Comparison of notes on book study of *Switch: How to Change Things when Change is Hard*[15] by Chip and Dan Heath. These notes are mine.

6.4 Further Tailoring the Process for Students

I realize that much of this chapter is written to the educator, and part of that is the importance of modeling these skills with our students and sharing our own experiences so they can learn from them. I also realize that while I have encouraged reading across the curriculum and a step-by-step process for a reader's notebook, I have not explicitly extended this work past the "teachersphere," and I want to make sure we can extend this beyond our own orbit. So I wanted to share some questions that I think will be helpful in having students make purposeful aesthetic decisions and share their own reader's notebooks with others:

- **Colors:** What colors did you choose? Why did you choose them? How do they relate to the mood, theme, or overall message of the book you read? How did you use color to determine hierarchy of text?

- **Icons and Drawings:** What icons and pictures did you draw? Did you draw these to highlight a relationship? How do these images add to, inform, and/or extend the content in the story or book?

- **Embellishments:** What embellishments (e.g., magazine pictures, online images, washi tape, stickers) did you use? Why did you choose these particular ones to inform and/or extend the content in the story or book?

- **Research:** What research was interesting to you? How might you use this research in your own writing?

- **Lexicon Library:** What words and/or phrases were interesting to you? Do you see any patterns and/or trends in the types of words and/or phrases you selected? How might you use these words and/or phrases in your own writing?

- **Quotes:** What quotes did you choose? Do you see any patterns and/or trends in the type of quotes you selected? Were there any chapters or parts of the book in which you struggled to find a good quote? If you could select one quote that best spoke to the essence of the book, what would it be?

The questions above can be used as journaling prompts for students, used to spark conversation in student groups, and/or as one-on-one prompts as students discuss their reading with their teacher. We have done a similar activity with secondary students and a sketch-noting exercise. The real meat of the learning is in these questions and how students compare and contrast their selections and design choices with other students. It's also in how they justify their specific selections of research, phrases, quotes, and design choices of color and visuals. I should also mention that this shouldn't be a "who did it better?" exercise. It is more important to have rich discussions about what one student included and perhaps another student didn't and what that says about their personal stance and interpretation of the reading. You can discuss why one student chose red and another blue to depict a quote or scene and what meaning that color added to the overall comprehension of that quote.

6.5 Planning Ahead

Beyond reading summaries, additional items that can be added to a reader's notebook are a list of books you have read (Figure 6.10) and a list of books to read next (Figure 6.11). I keep a running tally for the year. I have to say, it is such a sense of accomplishment to see a list of all the books at the end of the year. It also takes a lot of pressure off me when I finish a book, and I can simply glance at a list of five to seven books I already have in my possession that I can read next.

Figure 6.10 List of books I have read featuring stickers from
Harry Ransom Center and keyboard pic from Hanx Writer app

Lists of books aren't the only thing that can be added to a learner's
notebook. One could also add a list of topics that are interesting or
about which you want to know more and then determine what books,
TED Talks, and articles are needed to meet that thirst for knowledge.
As you can see in Figure 6.10, I have been most recently on a self-help
and mindfulness kick. Before that I had a long list of books, articles,
and resources that focused on note-taking and planners in the professional world.

Figure 6.11: List of books I want to read (that I already own)
with dates on which I finished reading each featuring dylusions
by Dyan Reaveley adhesive canvas and stickers

6.6 Taking Note of the Learner's Needs for the Notebook

This chapter is less about reading and more about what we do with what we consume and read. And it doesn't have to be books; it could be other media, such as articles, TED Talks, or even podcasts. Reading and scrapnoting ultimately lead to writing and learning. As I spent the last chapter on journaling and reflection (which is very kin to a writer's notebook but focuses more on an individual rather than the lens one uses to consume content), I didn't want to spend too much time on that here. Perhaps we can drop the idea of a reader's and/or writer's notebook in favor of a learner's notebook, digital or analog, and focus on what the learner does with what they consume and how they make sense of what they consume. Are they using the ideas and research they collect to better inform themselves as learners? Are they gathering information for a passion project or genius hour? Are they intending to publish an open letter or a blog post on a topic near and dear to them? While collecting and digesting content is important, it is equally as important to have a plan for what we do with this content.

I think sometimes we get tunnel vision and assume our options are limited to a sole technology, app, or device when in fact we have the world (both IRL and digital) at our fingertips. I realize this chapter may tip the scales towards analog, but I think it is leaning the scales towards purpose, choice, and crafting a process that works best for you and your students as learners. As you might imagine, when I asked my English teachers what tools their students used for a reader's notebook, some chose tools like Google Docs, and others chose a composition notebook. I find this is to be the case across multiple disciplines as well; for example, chemistry classes might use a quadrille-lined laboratory notebook with carbon copy ability, and an art history class might choose to keep their comparative analysis notes in the Notability app with dividers for each unit. While these notes are more academic and prescriptive than what a reader's notebook might be, I share them to highlight myriad avenues that are currently being taken just to take notes throughout the day. By no means am I saying all notes should reside in one app or tool; what I am saying is that a reader's or a learner's notebook should be far less prescriptive than the notes that are being taken in class. The reader's or learner's notebook should also afford the student more choice and customization because the tool is really for the leaner to document learning and things they want to learn.

All technologies have their limitations. That's why blending technologies is so fascinating to me (much like how I blend my handwritten notes with an interactive tool, using Thinglink and share photos
and videos of my analog notes on Instagram @NoteChef4u). No one
can say what the best tool is for you or your students; however, I do
think these topics will help lead you to consider a few things:

- **Accessibility:** My youngest son struggles with articulation
  and fine motor skills. For him, speech-to-text is not always
  accurate, and typing something is a chore and a barrier, but
  he is able to draw and handwrite his ideas with more comfort
  and effectiveness. For other students, speech-to-text and the
  keyboard might be integral to a student getting their message
  across. My point in mentioning this is that providing flexibil-
  ity in how students document and summarize their learning
  can allow students to express their learning in a way that is
  most meaningful to them.

- **Adding Value:** When I mention technology, please know that
  both a pencil or an iPad could be classified as such. The bigger question here is whatever technology is selected should at
  the very least enhance if not add value for the learner and to
  the ultimate goals of the project at hand. Allow your students
  to advocate for the technology that works best for them as a
  learner and the technology that makes most sense for the current project or endeavor.

- **Archival:** We still must be able to grade and collect work; I
  realize that. In the case of my son, he could take a picture of his
  writing and share it to his Google Drive portfolio.

Here's the bottom line: Use the best tool for the job, ensure that
whatever process students use to digest and make sense of content

has purpose, guide your students to learn from their notebooks, and devise a plan for action and further learning that extends beyond the content they consume and summarize.

AWESOME AMULET CHECKLIST

☐ My students read curricular and surprisingly educational texts.

☐ My students read and consume multiple modes of media (e.g., books, articles, podcasts, TED Talks).

☐ My students explore a balance of both analog and digital text.

☐ My students can use color to add meaning and to define hierarchy and relationships of content they have read.

☐ My students can use visuals and icons to add meaning to content they have read.

☐ My students can purposefully embellish their reader's notebook entries with analog and/or digital artifacts like images, shapes, and ephemera that add to and extend the meaning of their book summaries.

☐ My students can select meaningful research from the book and justify their selections.

☐ My students can discover and archive words and phrases that have personal meaning to them throughout a text or piece of media.

☐ My students can locate quotes from the book that are personally or academically relevant to them and incorporate them within their reader's notebook.

☐ My students can have productive conversations with other students about their reader's notebooks selections.

☐ My students can apply these research studies and exemplars (e.g., quotes and words and phrases) to their own writing.

☐ My students can advocate for the best tool/technology for a project or assignment and determine when certain tools add value and when they don't.

WAKEFUL WHIMSY CORE IDEAS

- **English Language Arts:** Have students research color psychology and adapt it to a quote, passage, a poem, or a song.

- **Math and Science:** Have students choose a formula, theorem, force, or process and translate it entirely into a visual equation or a series of emojis. Have students share these with their peers and see if they can guess what they are. Ones that weren't easily guessed or needed heavy explanations should then be revised for clarity.

- **Social Studies:** Have students bring in a tangible item or piece of ephemera (e.g., library card, photograph, a postcard, etc.) and connect it to a quote, historical figure, or time period. What was its significance? How has it changed? How has it remained the same?

SHARE YOUR OWN EXAMPLES AND IDEAS INSPIRED BY THIS CHAPTER. BE SURE TO TAG YOUR COMMENTS: #CREATIVELYPRODUCTIVE.

Citations

1. Harris, Michael. "I have forgotten how to read." *The Globe and Mail*. February 9, 2018. theglobeandmail.com/opinion/i-have-forgotten-how-toread/article37921379.

2. Sullivan, Patrick. "An Open Letter to High School Students about Reading | AAUP." *Aaup.org*. May–June 2016. aaup.org/article/open-letter-high-school-students-about-reading#.W80hPa2ZOu4.

3. Paul, Annie. "Reading Literature Makes Us Smarter and Nicer." *TIME.com*. June 3, 2013. ideas.time.com/2013/06/03/why-we-should-read-literature.

4. Newhouse, Kara. "How Reading Novels in Math Class Can Strengthen Student Engagement." *KQED.org*. March 18, 2018. kqed.org/mindshift/50640/how-reading-novels-in-math-class-can-strengthen-student-engagement.

5. Diakiw, Jerry. "Reading and Life Success." *HuffPost Canada*. May 4, 2017. huffingtonpost.ca/jerry-diakiw/reading-and-life-success_b_16404148.html.

6. Douglas, Jonathan. "The Importance of Instilling a Need to Read." *Telegraph.co.uk*. May 4, 2013. telegraph.co.uk/education/educationopinion/10035473/The-importance-of-instilling-a-need-to-read.html.

7. Crowe, Kelsey & McDowell, Emily. *There Is No Good Card for This*. New York, New York: HarperOne, 2017.

8. Kleon, Austin. "The importance of revisiting notebooks – Austin Kleon – Medium." *Medium*. December 17, 2017. medium.com/@austinkleon/the-importance-of-revisiting-notebooks-51f6d1309a78.

9. Hopkins, Ellen. *Crank*. New York, New York: Margaret K. McElderry Books, 2004.

10. Smit, Irene, and Irene van der Hulst. *A Book That Takes Its Time*. New York, New York: Workman Publishing Company, 2017.

11. Dickinson, Emily, Marta L. Werner, and Jen Bervin. *Envelope Poems*. New York: New Directions, 2016.

12. Alter, Adam. "Why our screens make us less happy." *Ted.com*. ted.com/talks/adam_alter_why_our_screens_make_us_less_happy?language=en.

13. Stanier, Michael Bungay. *The Coaching Habit*. Toronto, Ontario: Box of Crayons Press, 2016.

14. Leitman, Margot. 2015. *Long story short*. Sasquatch Books.

15. Heath, Chip & Heath, Dan. *Switch*. London: Random House Business, 2011.

Research

- Holiday, Ryan. 2017. Perennial Seller. London: Profile Books.
- Kleon, Austin. 2017. "Guardian spirits." Austinkleon.com. austinkleon.com/2017/12/12/guardian-spirits-2
- Kleon, Austin. 2014. Show your work!. Workman Publishing Company.
- Kleon, Austin. 2012. Steal like an artist. 1st arg. Workman Publishing Company.
- Krogerus, Mikael; Tschäppeler, Roman & Piening, Jenny. 2012. The decision book. New York: W.W. Norton & Co.
- Rigal, Emily-Anne. 2015. FLAWD. Penguin Publishing Group.

WORKING WISDOMS
A Few More Things to Know before You Go

I am part Italian. I love a good Italian meal, and gnocchi is one of my faves. It is a hearty potato dumpling, and it is simply divine. I tend to treat my PD resources and creations the same way. I know the adage "less is more," but sometimes I think, *more is more.* Now with a hearty Italian dish, you will probably dive right in, and then once you become full, set it aside. But if you are like me, you don't let that delectable dish out of your sight. And once you are ready to dig back in, you do just that. Perhaps you munch on a breadstick or two. Maybe you have another glass of wine and don't return to that gnocchi that evening. You request a to-go bag and return to it the next day. But the point is, you have something to which you can return that repeatedly fills you up and fuels you. If you made it through all six chapters, you might already be full. Full of ideas, full of action items, full of inspiration. So feel free to dine on these morsels now or return to them as you need additional inspiration or fuel.

My first book, *Cultivating Communication in the Classroom: Future-Ready Skills for Secondary Students*, like this one, was college- and career-ready focused, so I sought to add one more layer. Both books highlight tips, ideas, and best practices from students, educators, and professionals from around the world. I could have stopped there, but I felt there was more to say on these topics. Rather than disrupt the flow of the chapters, I decided to include the responses to several pertinent questions as an additional resource.

As we don't know what paths our students will take in life, I chose people from all walks of life pursuing a variety of diverse professions. Below I have curated thoughtful responses from people in companies with which you and your students might be familiar: Book Creator, BrainPop, bulb, Edmodo, and Explain Everything as well as a variety of professions. Professions range from architects, marketing consultants, makeup and hair artists to real estate CEO's, nurses, and sought-after authors and designers. As you would imagine, their responses to the following questions vary quite a bit, and that is kind of the point. There is no singular locator ring for success; there are many. And to be a perennial pupil, there are a variety of pathways to follow. I think you will find some similar threads within these responses. I toyed with the idea of removing similar responses but ended up keeping them, as many came from different professions, and I thought it would be valuable to see that values tend to align across a variety of otherwise dissimilar professions. There are people who don't learn these lessons until many years on the job and others who end up paying a life or business coach inordinate amounts of money; thus, I found it difficult to weed responses because it almost felt like removing gold from a treasure chest. In the end, I plucked the best and most thoughtful responses regardless of the fields from which they came and included them below.

Finally, I want to mention that this wasn't a random survey. I have a professional or personal relationship with all the people listed below. Some are colleagues. Some are people with whom I have done business. Some I engage with on social media. Some are family. In true TechChef4u fashion, my goal was to create recipes that would inspire you to action and to eventually remix and make your own. Think about the people you know and the people in your lives and your students' lives and how their insights could be valuable—dare I say invaluable—to your students. Twenty-three professionals completed this survey. And if you consider that many of these people have been in their respective fields for more than a decade—and some of them for up to fifty years—their collected expertise is unparalleled. I am indeed overwhelmed by the amassed knowledge of these individuals, and I hope that their tips, strategies, and best practices prove to be as divine and delectable as I found them to be no matter when you choose to dine on them.

How do you keep your work organized electronically?

Use Folders and Labels

"For mail, it's all about folders and labels. When something comes to my inbox, I delete it if I don't need it, or I put it in a folder if no action beyond reading it is required. If an action is required, I do one of two things: If I think it can be addressed quickly without disrupting what I was already working on too much, I address it right there and then move it to a folder. If I can't address it quickly, I create a time block on my calendar for it and then move it to a folder. Either way, the message is cleared from my inbox!"

—**Reshan Richards**, Co-founder of Explain Everything

Organize by Clients and Companies

"I have them all in files/folders—by clients and companies I work or have worked for."

—Judy Jacomino, makeup and hair artist

Store Content in Colored Folders

"I like to use colored folders and name each file, which is stored in one service."

—Mary Johnson, charge nurse RN

Separate Personal and Work Folders

"I separate personal files from work files. I keep files for separate clients in separate folders, with each of them organized into categories in that folder; in addition, each of the files starts with a specific one- to three-letter prefix to indicate which client it belongs to."

—Peter Nevland, marketing consultant/spoken word performer

Curate Digital Links with Padlet

"I create Padlets for almost everything! I love being able to add digital links directly to my Padlet from my phone."

—Audrey O'Clair, independent contractor
in education consulting

Star Folders and Use Specific Naming Conventions

"I don't use colour coding, but I do have starred folders, and I have well-structured and named folders (backed up to Dropbox so it's accessible on any device). I use Basecamp for managing longer-term projects with tasks, but on a daily basis I will often just use the Notes app on Mac to write a to-do list, which I can delete when finished."

—Dan Kemp, Book Creator community manager

Organize Email Folders

"I have different folders in my email that help me keep track of emails easily."

—Whitney Woodard, founder/CEO of Beaded by W

Use Categories and Key Words

"(1) I use keyword searches mostly. So I make sure I name items with keywords that I anticipate I would search. (2) I use folders in Google Drive. I want everything accessible from any device anywhere, so Google Drive is where I put all my documents. (3) Email is my other place I store work. I don't delete anything. I don't use folders in email, but I do use three categories to mark emails for follow-up: (a) unread, (b) star for I need to respond, (c) important—meaning this is something I will refer to soon."

—Bria Jones, head of customer care at bulb

Use Email as a To-Do list

"I use my email inbox as a to-do list, leaving emails in there until they're dealt with. I also leverage Trello from time to time."

—Michael Crawford, director of strategy and partnerships

Categorize for Organization

"Everything is organized in categories (program, semester, operations, etc.) on Google Drive, then I aim for zero emails in my inbox and also organize my emails into categories."

—Sabina Bharwani, founder, K12 CS education organization

Use a Blend of Folders, Subfolders, and SMART Notebooks

"I use Google Drive for all documents. All documents are organized into folders and subfolders. For old-schoolers like me or for those that just like to use pen and notebooks, I've recently started using the Rocketbook Everlast notebook. It's just a wire bound, environmentally friendly "smart" notebook that uses special paper you can write your notes on. Then you scan your pages using the Rocketbook app, and it converts it into a PDF and automatically sends it out to various apps, such as Evernote, Google Drive, Slack, Dropbox, OneNote, or your email."

—Melissa Johnson, real estate CEO

What are your strategies for managing your time and avoiding distractions?

Use Two Inboxes

"I have two inboxes (mac mail for work, webmail for everything else), and in both cases I maintain inbox zero using folders/labels. I also plan my day using my calendar, blocking off time for stuff I want to do and logging the time when I did something I hadn't originally planned."

—Reshan Richards, chief learning officer, Explain Everything Inc.

Select One Project at a Time

"When I am alone, I can really focus on what I need to get done. I know I have allotted time for me before family comes into play. So my main strategy is when I am alone, I use it to its full potential, sticking to one project at a time and finishing it."

—Judy Jacomino, makeup and hair artist

Prioritize Urgency

"I prioritize in terms of urgency but not in a first-come-first-serve order. Family matters usually come first. Distractions are unavoidable, especially with small kids. I just manage them as part of the equation and as they come. I worked as a mountain guide many years ago. Our mantra was 'Scramble be Flexible.' That applies to everything I do, but when it comes to needing or carving 'uninterrupted time,' staying up late and working at night is a last (avoid if possible) resource."

—Efraín E. Vélez, architect

Predetermine Goals and Urgency

"Know goals ahead of time, close doors to office, put in headphones, listen to music with no lyrics, do the important stuff first whether it's urgent or not."

—Peter Nevland, marketing consultant/spoken word performer

Work in Short Bursts

"I work in short bursts of two to three hours when I know I will be productive and focused. If I find myself drifting off or checking social media, I know it's time to stop, take a break, and come back later."

—Dan Kemp, Book Creator community manager

Schedule Work Time

"Schedule work on calendar or list. I often email myself if I'm away from work, and I think of ideas or other priorities on my to-do list. Document clearly what product is my goal or what I want to have happen when I am done."

—Demetrius Lewis, professional development specialist, Texas Education Agency

Work in Thirty-Minute Increments

"I plan my day out in thirty-minute increments and avoid large chunks of free time. If something takes longer than planned, that is just fine, but in order for me to stay focused, I need to have time set aside for deep work. I save my most important tasks for early morning when I'm fresh and leave more mindless work for the end of the day. Working from home, it can be challenging to ignore house projects to get work done, so if it is written in the calendar, I tend to follow through more."

—**Audrey O'Clair**, independent contractor
in education consulting

Prioritize, Delegate, and Reflect

"This is a tricky one! My time is in extremely high demand, so it is paramount that I am able to prioritize. First and foremost, I make time at the beginning of every day to plan my day as best as possible—setting aside time on my calendar to address work that can be done uninterrupted, delegating work to my team, and making the difficult decisions around what can be delayed or put off until tomorrow; additionally, I set aside time to reflect back on each day to ensure I feel good about what was accomplished (even if I didn't make it through my to-do list), where I could have improved, and starting to think about what needs to be addressed the following day. Also, I use the Eisenhower Decision Matrix to determine what is urgent and important (needs immediate attention), what is important but not urgent (can be dealt with tomorrow), urgent but not important, and lastly neither urgent nor important."

—**Jacob Hanson**, managing partner, PR with Panache!
(PR and integrated marketing)

Prioritize and Remove Distractions

"(1) I use a chrome extension called Momentum to type my big priorities for the day. (2) When working on a project that needs my brain fully engaged, I am very disciplined to not check my email, which will distract me and take me off task. If it is urgent, my team knows to text or slack me. (3) I am always working ahead, as I know projects come up unexpectedly daily. (4) With any project, I spend time up-front evaluating the requirements so that I can best estimate the time it will take to accomplish. (5) Most importantly, I schedule time in my calendar to complete tasks, or else my calendar will fill up with meetings, and I won't be able to get things done."

—**Bria Jones**, head of customer care at bulb

Plan Brain Dumps and Select Environments for Success

"For managing my time and staving off distractions, I do a few things: First, I establish the things I need to do, and I prioritize them. I use the 6-Step Brain Dump tool (available for download at techchef4u.com/book). I then enter the prioritized tasks into my calendar. Second, I determine the type of environment I need to accomplish the tasks. Sometimes I need solitude. Sometimes I need teammates. Based on the type of task and its due date, I go where I need to go. Third, I put my phone on vibrate; I close my email tab; I get out of Slack. If I don't remove the potential for distraction, I will get distracted. It's inevitable."

—**Michael Crawford**, director of strategy and partnerships

Manage and Break Down Tasks

"I organize my day in Asana—a task management system that basically follows the GTD (getting things done) protocol developed by David Allen. Each project has its "space," and the team breaks down the objectives into small achievable goals. Each goal can be assigned and dated, so not only do I keep myself accountable, I can see how the team does too."

—**Andrew Gardner**, VP professional learning, BrainPOP

Conduct Short Meetings with Clear Action Items

"Conduct short meetings (typically not longer than thirty minutes). Have clear action items. Have strategic ("blue-sky") meetings once a quarter or so, ideally offsite. Try not to check email during meetings."

—**Manish Kothari**, general manager at Edmodo (in charge of revenue and business development)

Discover Analog and Digital Distraction Busters

"(1) I turn off all notifications on my phone for all social media. I also place in "do not disturb" mode when working on projects that need my full concentration. (2) I've learned that simply closing my door while I'm focusing on a project is very effective when I can't afford to be interrupted. My team knows that if the door is closed, unless it's an emergency, DO NOT DISTURB! (3) I use Google Calendar to block off time for appointments and meetings. This way I don't overcommit myself. (4) I use Toggl, which is a time-keeping app available on your desktop and phone. (They also have a Chrome extension for quick access). I use this to track the time I spend on specific projects throughout the day. I track time spent in meetings, checking email, strategic planning, etc. It's been a great tool for tracking where I am being efficient (or sometimes not efficient) with my time. I also have my team using it so that I use it as a management tool. It allows me to see where they are spending the most time and ensures that our processes are efficient and effective. Toggl also has a reporting feature that allows you to see your whole team's time in one place!"

—Melissa Johnson, real estate CEO

Stave Off Distractions during Creative Work

"I move physically to a place that will lessen my distractions. As counterintuitive as this sounds, I move away from my desk because that's also where I handle house management and bills etc., and it can be tempting to me to distract myself away from my writing and/or creative obligations. I reason to myself, *See? I'm still doing something important,* and will justify not doing the important creative work I need to do. I also will go to cafes that don't have internet access if I'm doing intensive creative work so that I won't be tempted to surf the web when I'm feeling snagged. If something comes up that I need to research while I'm creating, I write in my notebook to Google it later when I'm back online and leave a space for it in my writing."

—Kayla Cagan, author and freelance writer (content creation, social media, etc.)

Separate Your Work Spaces

"Working from a home office can be very easily distracting, so I suggest having a work space separate from your living spaces. Use another room in the house if you can spare it, or perhaps a corner of a room where the work doesn't leave. I find that if I bring my work to the couch with me, the only thing I will achieve is watching television."

—James Burke, owner of mixed media arts business in e-commerce and social media

What is your process or protocol for SHARED digital notes and/or agendas?

Ensure Privacy with View-Only Notes

"The digital notes/programs I have used allow others access to view only. As these are medical documents, only the author of the note is allowed access to make any changes, and that is limited also."

—Mary Johnson, charge nurse RN

Set Parameters for Collaborative Note-Taking and Digital Whiteboards

"We are trying to do more collaborative note-taking on digital whiteboards. It requires a different set of parameters and structures than something that is more linear like a Google Doc or a note in Evernote. It is helpful if someone takes ownership of doing cleanup/organizing/synthesis on behalf of others after a collaborative note-taking session."

—Reshan Richard, Co-founder of Explain Everything

Clearly State Agendas

"Notes are typically taken by a project manager and/or a designated assistant. Ideally, agendas are clearly stated prior to having a meeting, although in my experience, that is rarely the case. Digitally, for sharing, there are many tools out there for this. My current office uses Basecamp, but in the past, I've used Intranet systems, Dropbox, Outlook, and/or regular email."

—Efraín E. Vélez, architect

Be Cognizant of Permissions and Intellectual Property

"We always use Google sheets/docs. The nature of the content being shared dictates what permissions we give the folks we are sharing with (view only, etc.). Additionally, we have to ensure that no intellectual property flows between two clients or between our internal client teams, so keeping this information siloed is an absolute must for our company."

—**Jacob Hanson**, managing partner, PR with Panache!
(PR and integrated marketing)

Email Important Points

"Right now I don't have a process for this, as I very rarely take "formal" notes from meetings. Most likely I will capture notes with pen and paper, then email any important points or assigned tasks after the meeting. I used to work as an administrator where taking minutes was integral to my job, and using a specific, consistent format which I developed over time was crucial."

—**Dan Kemp**, Book Creator community manager

Use Google Docs Efficiently

"I use Google Docs with the date of the latest meeting first."

—**Danny Johnson**, founder, Freedom Driven LLC

Create Shared Templates

"Create a shared template and add to the document as the meeting is happening."

—**Audrey O'Clair**, independent contractor
in education consulting

Assign Agenda Roles

"One person builds the agenda, others add to it, and the moderator prioritizes items for discussion."

—Cynthia Perkins, technology specialist in education, editor for Franchise Operations Manuals

Use Agendas to Assign Project

"We use Asana to develop agendas for meetings. Once the item has been discussed and assigned, we categorize it within one of the projects, and it gets completed in a timely way."

—Andrew Gardner, VP professional learning, BrainPOP

Determine the Ws

"At the beginning of the meeting, we determine who will be taking notes, on what doc, and where that doc will live. Who, what, and where are determined by the nature of the meeting."

—Michael Crawford, director of strategy and partnerships

Use a Meeting Scorecard

"We use Slack for in-house communications, which allows us to track messages, notes, and file sharing. In our meetings, we use a "meeting scorecard" that is prefilled by one person and shared at the meeting. After the meeting, the meeting leader scans and shares with everyone on the team. This way we can take notes on specific action items for ourselves and not have to worry about writing every single thing down."

—Melissa Johnson, real estate CEO

What are your best practices (or processes) for setting and achieving personal and professional goals?

Set Small Goals to Reach Big Goals

"When I have a professional or personal goal, I like to stick to small achievements at a time. Setting smaller goals to reach the bigger goal is key for me; for example, I work and practice a bit today, then tomorrow I can do that same small goal quicker, and so on."

—**Judy Jacomino**, makeup and hair artist

Design for Living

"I 'design' for a living. That means I practice a day-to-day methodology that enables me not only to set goals and/or targets but also trace and modify course(s) depending on constraints, setbacks, and timing. Design is about having a clear 'performative' goal/intent rather than a 'prescribed'/specific one. This enables me to be happy whenever I'm able to fulfill a task that meets my intent rather than a specific, rigid/forced outcome."

—**Efraín E. Vélez**, architect

Focus with Accountability

"I find accountability very important. If I set goals for myself, by myself—I'm unlikely to stick to them. But if I set objectives in collaboration with colleagues or friends/family, that accountability helps me stay focused."

—**Dan Kemp**, Book Creator community manager

Set SMART Goals

"I like to use the SMART goal framework for setting goals: Specific Measurable Attainable Relevant Timely. These goals do not all need to be big, lofty goals; they could be as simple as managing time more effectively, improving electronic communication, or getting up a little earlier in the morning! One of my goals is that I am always learning, so I schedule learning time every single day. It might be five minutes one day or sixty the next, but I strive to read a blog post, listen to a podcast, attend a webinar, or even just have a conversation with a team member to learn more about something they have expertise in."

—Jacob Hanson, managing partner, PR with Panache!
(PR and integrated marketing)

Plan on Sundays

"Setting yearly goals, then breaking down by quarter and then by current month, then planning each week on Sunday keeps my weekly work aligned with my goals for the year."

—Danny Johnson, founder, Freedom Driven LLC

Goal Set with the Innovator's Compass

"I use the Innovator's Compass (innovatorscompass.org) to set goals for individual projects and long-term goals (e.g., New Year's Resolutions/Reflections). I am not afraid of a little healthy procrastination."

—Audrey O'Clair, independent contractor in education consulting

Turn to a Life and/or Business Coach

"I have a life coach that I meet with every other week, and we go over where I am in life and where I want to go, and she helps me manage my stress. I also have a business coach that visits with me quarterly; we go over budget and my P&L. Having secondary people in your life that are not working for your business that will make you set goals and call you on your BS is very important!"

—**Chelle Neff**, founder, Urban Betty

Create Visualizations for Your Goals

"I create visuals (mind maps) or sketch out what I want to achieve. I make the goal real to me. I seek out mentors or advisors who have been there or have achieved what I am trying to accomplish. I also tie the goal to some real benefit that matters to me in the future."

—**Demetrius Lewis**, professional development specialist,
Texas Education Agency

Focus on Weekly Goals on Monday Mornings

"I set weekly goals and review Monday morning. Most often I need to rearrange, delete, and add so it is a living document."

—**Deb Evans**, social media consultant in franchising

Create a Goal Portfolio

"I use my bulb portfolio as a special place to write my goals and go back and collect evidence of what I'm doing to improve or attain my goals. I also regularly reflect on my goals in my portfolio."

—**Bria Jones**, head of customer care at bulb

Take Breaks and Be Mindful

"I take regular breaks, meditate, and mark off time in the calendar specifically toward completing tasks on a project."

—**Andrew Gardner**, VP professional learning, BrainPOP

Approach Goal Setting with a Framework

"While I don't do these regularly (although I'm working on it!), there are a few strategies I suggest: (1) the popular one, SMART goals (mindtools.com/pages/article/smart-goals.htm). Even a cursory understanding of this framework can help one consider, articulate, and establish valuable goals. (2) WOOP (characterlab.org/woop). Backed by solid research, WOOP is an excellent approach to both setting goals and overcoming the predictable challenges one will face."

—Michael Crawford, director of strategy and partnerships

Quantify Goals

"Track/quantify them; for example, I have a goal to visit one CS classroom per two weeks outside of Hello World; I have a goal to not eat refined sugar for thirty days."

—Sabina Bharwani, founder, K12 CS education organization

Set Twelve-Week Goals

"At the beginning of the year, I always set my personal goals and my business goals. After I started working with a business coach, I realized that these two things must align to achieve true success and to create purposeful goals that really move you to your overall vision of your life. In the office, our team has begun implementing the twelve-week year, which is based on the premise that we are most motivated to achieve our goals when it's "crunch time" as the year winds down. By setting your major goal and breaking it down into twelve weeks, you are able to accomplish more in shorter periods of time and have more immediate gratification. It really turns the idea of the calendar year into something more manageable."

—Melissa Johnson, real estate CEO

Be Accountable to Yourself with Goal-Setting Questions

"I try to do my intense creative work first thing in the morning, then management and admin work, then work I call thoughtless work (like walking the dog; it doesn't take a lot mentally to do that). Now, that doesn't always work out scheduling wise, and if I'm working with a client, or if I'm on a deadline with my publisher, this all has to shift around to focus my attention on what's most pressing. I also ask myself the following questions to keep me going. I found this list a while back and I can't remember the source, unfortunately: (1) Am I following my curiosity? (2) Am I working with honor and dignity? (3) Am I doing the best work I can at the moment? (4) Am I being respectful to the people who put me in this position? (5) Am I being kind to people?"

—**Kayla Cagan**, author and freelance writer
(content creation, social media, etc.)

Be Reflective in Your Goal Setting

"I keep more short-term, realistically achievable goals in the forefront of my mind and the bigger ones as dreams in the back. Being able to meet these short-term goals more frequently provides a boost of motivation to reach the next one. My work in content creation is very open ended, so sometimes setting a specific goal doesn't really benefit the process. It's also not enough to say my goal is to "be better," because that is a given. If ever I feel lost for direction, I will look at the last hurdle I just jumped over and where I'm at now and ask, *What could I do with that last success?* One path will generally lead you down another, and before you know it, you have a new direction and goal."

—**James Burke**, owner of mixed media arts business
in e-commerce and social media

If you could give our current middle school or high school students one piece of advice for the future, what would it be?

Organize Your Hours

"Organize your hours so you address what needs to be done first, creating more time for the things that you enjoy doing."

—**Reshan Richard**, Co-founder of Explain Everything

Don't Waste Time

"Your time is your currency. Don't waste your time, don't waste other people's time, and don't let your time be devalued by distractions that don't bring you joy or energy. How you spend your minutes is how you spend your days, and how you spend your days is how you spend your life. GREAT LUCK TO YOU!"

—**Kayla Cagan**, author and freelance writer (content creation, social media, etc.)

Tackle Life's Hurdles

"Unfortunately there will be assignments, classes, and studying that has to happen even if a student does not care for that particular subject. Try your hardest in those classes because in life there will always be courses and paths that we will not like, but we have to get through those hurdles to get to where we really want to be. Middle and high school are preparation for the endurance and tolerance we will need for life."

—**Judy Jacomino**, makeup and hair artist

Plan with Purpose

"Plan ahead and have a clear purpose but stay flexible along the way. Wonderful things happen when you allow purpose to be positively enriched. Beware of negative influences. Understand that means, methods, and language always change and that purpose dies if it is not modified (or constantly redefined) in tandem with those external influences."

—Efraín E. Vélez, architect

Be Committed

"You will have thousands of great, important or hugely profitable ideas in your life. You will only benefit from the ones you commit to and organize so that you can access them again and again and again."

—Peter Nevland, marketing consultant/spoken word performer

Know That Popularity and Grades are Fleeting

"Being popular won't get you the job you are looking for, nor will arguing for a grade. Neither of those things are brought into consideration in the professional world."

—Jacob Hanson, managing partner, PR with Panache!
(PR and integrated marketing)

Work Smart

"Work smart. It's not the length of time you spend on something that matters; it's how focused you are when working at it. Find the conditions that help you concentrate on what you're doing. (Do you need to listen to music? Maybe you need total quiet? Do you like to work alone or surrounded by others? How much light do you need around you?)"

—Dan Kemp, Book Creator community manager

Find Role Models

"Find good role models! Study how people work and behave! Be kind."

—**Audrey O'Clair**, independent contractor
in education consulting

Take a Day-by-Day Approach

"Don't worry about the future; just do the best thing you can do for yourself today. Everything that you plan will always change."

—**Chelle Neff**, founder, Urban Betty

Manage Yourself

"Learn self-management techniques to handle distractions and sometimes failure. Know there is a "next play" to be prepared for. Whoever adjusts and prepares in the most efficient manner will be better prepared to take advantage of the next opportunity."

—**Demetrius Lewis**, professional development specialist,
Texas Education Agency

Ask Questions

"Do not be afraid to ask questions; you can learn SO much from other people!"

—**Whitney Woodard**, founder/CEO, Beaded by W

Manage Your Time and Prioritize Your Tasks

"Time management and prioritizing tasks is one of the most challenging things in the business world. There is always too much to do and not enough time. Use your schoolwork to practice this skill. Try different methods until you find one that works well for you. You alone are responsible for this. Don't rely on your teacher or parents to give you reminders to help you to manage your time and tasks. Take ownership of your work. If you can be successful in managing your time well, you are setting yourself up for success in any career."

—**Bria Jones**, head of customer care at bulb

Do You

"It is OK to try something and find it is boring (or to fail). Don't get caught up with what others are doing."

—**Manish Kothari**, general manager at Edmodo
(in charge of revenue and business development)

Seek Goals, Not a Profession

"Professionally, focus on goals, not a profession (i.e., 'I want to help people learn' rather than 'I want to be a teacher.'"

—**Andrew Gardner**, VP professional learning, BrainPOP

Control What You Can Control

"Control what you can control. Too often we burn a ton of fuel worrying and stressing about things in the past, things in the future, or things we can't control. There are tools and strategies that everyone has access to that can increase the likelihood that the life that unfolds resembles the life one seeks. By being mindful of the things we can control in our lives and by taking steps in service of those things, we give ourselves the best chance of living our best lives."

—**Michael Crawford**, director of strategy and partnerships

Be Resourceful

"People think that in order to do the types of things they're interested in (journalism, AI programming, be a chef, etc.), they need a job at a certain place. You can do these things without the job; you just need to be resourceful and not let time get away from you."

—**Sabina Bharwani**, founder, K12 CS education organization

Be Adaptable

"It's so cliché, but be ADAPTABLE! When I took 'Business Studies,' there wasn't even a social media component, which is now my main source of marketing and passive revenue streams. Another piece of advice I've always held on to was 'not everything has to work out.' Some of my biggest successes have come hot off the heels of my biggest disappointments . . . such is the nature of life; it ebbs and flows. If you're adaptable and dedicated, you will be completely fine."

—**James Burke**, owner of mixed media arts business in e-commerce and social media

Stay Organized and Seek What Works for You

"Find what works best for you to stay organized. There are so many ways to do this now! If you're tech minded, managing your time might be easier using reminders and apps. For creative types, bullet journals or planners might be the way to go. There's no right or wrong way to do this. I use a combination of both, but what works for me might not work for the next person. Experiment!"

—**Melissa Johnson**, real estate CEO

Use Time Wisely

"There is not one perfect formula or approach, but ultimately time is the scarcest resource, and habits around using time wisely will serve a learner of any age well for the rest of their lives."

—**Reshan Richard**, Co-founder of Explain Everything

Strengthen Your Soft Skills

"What works for me may not work for anyone else. These skills are essential in our workplace and should not be overlooked. As a business owner and someone who plays a role in our hiring process, cultural fit is one of the most important factors in choosing the right applicant. A large part of figuring that out is evaluating their soft skills, not so much about their experience."

—**Jacob Hanson**, managing partner, PR with Panache!
(PR and integrated marketing)

Seek Clarity

"If you don't have clarity on what you really want, completing goals that don't align with you won't be fulfilling."

—**Danny Johnson**, founder, Freedom Driven LLC

Foster Internal Habits

"Time management, organization skills, and goal-setting are excellent ideas and something that is practical and will certainly be used. The ones who are able to adapt to these habits and make them internal will have a greater advantage tomorrow."

—**Demetrius Lewis**, professional development specialist,
Texas Education Agency

Set Big Goals

"Don't ever be afraid to set big goals for yourself. Take the time to really think about what you want—be specific! Visualize what it would look like and feel like to accomplish that goal. You can use apps like Canva to create a vision board for yourself to stay focused on your goal, then break it down into smaller actionable items. Anything you do—no matter how small—that moves you closer to your goal will be worth it!"

—Melissa Johnson, real estate CEO

Follow Your Passions and Find a Tribe

"Follow what you're passionate about: sports, art, music, theater, social justice, the environment, reading, or anything else healthy and positive. If you're not getting enough of what you love at your school, do it after school. Form your own clubs and find the people who love what you do and geek out about it together. Your happiness will skyrocket."

—Kayla Cagan, author and freelance writer
(content creation, social media, etc.)

Those who know me say I have a "Lisa finger." I call it the "Yes, and . . ." finger. It is basically when a topic comes up in discussion, and I raise my index finger and say, "Yes, AND let's do this" or "Yes, AND what about this?" So with these professional nuggets, I thought I would share one more idea. Sure, these are meant as inspiration, guidance for your students, and perhaps justification and validation for practices you are already doing with your students, but there are a few other ideas that one could do with this list:

RESEARCH

Research (personally or with your students and/or PLN) some of the tools and processes mentioned. A few of the tools that initially came to mind for me were Asana, bulb, Momentum, Padlet, Slack, Trello, and the Rocketbook Everlast Notebook. Some of the practices and processes mentioned were Blue Sky Meetings, the Eisenhower Decision Matrix, the Getting Things Done protocol, the Innovator's Compass, the SMART goal framework, Timeboxing, and the WOOP activity.

LIST the SIMILARITIES

Locate similar threads from multiple professions. The lead-ins to each quote should make that easy. From there, create a list of the top five to ten strategies that resonate with you and/or your students, the strategies you would like to pursue and practice and/or adapt for your students to pursue and practice.

PRACTICE with PURPOSE

Consider forming groups or teams that test out some of the strategies and report back.

And finally, share you ideas, innovations, and adaptations using the #creativelyproductive hashtag.

People to Follow

Throughout the book, I have talked about interesting and intriguing people to follow on Instagram. I've mentioned quite a few throughout the book, but you can find an ever-growing list online at techchef4u.com/book. As many of these skills and products shared throughout the book are highly visual, it only makes sense that these individuals would choose the most visual social media platform to share their ideas and insights. While the list encompasses Instagrammers, check out their bios. Many of them have YouTube channels, Etsy stores where they offer analog and digital downloads and templates, and websites with blogs where they dig deeper into the ideas and topics from their feed.

TECHCHEF4U.COM/BOOKS

BRING LISA JOHNSON TO YOUR SCHOOL OR DISTRICT

Lisa Johnson has more than eighteen years of educational experience ranging from teaching high school English and middle school math to international curriculum development, creating and presenting workshops, and even running technology integration camps across the state. She has been published in respected online entities like Edutopia, SmartBrief, and Corwin Connect and has been included in both editions of *iPads in Education for Dummies* as well as *The Missing Voices in Ed Tech*.

Currently Lisa serves as an Educational Technologist for Eanes ISD, which proudly supports a 1:1 iPad initiative for K–12. She was also recognized and selected as an Apple Distinguished Educator in 2013 and Lead PBS Digital Innovator for the state of Texas in 2016. As an author, curriculum writer, Ed Tech for a K–12 1:1 iPad district, and a mother of two mobile natives, Lisa has the ability to see and share how tools and technologies (both analog and digital) can impact and redefine pedagogy and instruction in the classroom and impact students long after they leave our classrooms. Bringing her unique home blend of purposeful pedagogy and perspective, Lisa empowers educators with critical ingredients and timeless techniques to cook up a new recipe for learning. She has delivered thoughtful keynotes, inspiring sessions, and interactive workshops to educators at campuses and conferences all over the world. Here are some of her most popular session topics:

Bonkers for Bullet Journals

This session highlights the recent trend of bullet journaling (which is essentially a mash-up of a planner, to-do list, sketchbook, writer/reader's notebook, and diary) and shares ideas for how you can set goals using habit and goal trackers for fitness, study, sleep, nutrition, etc. If you have a bullet journal, please bring it to show and tell!

Building Competency with Student Base Camps

How do you ensure that all students are successful in experiencing the legitimate instructional functionality of the iPad AND achieve a technical baseline of skills? iPad Base Camps, of course! Come learn and experience firsthand what an iPad Base Camp is and best practices for conducting one. Participants will leave with a toolkit of resources that support a variety of types of iPad Base Camps as well as logistical tips and structures for communication, process, and organization for delivering large-scale PD to secondary students. (A fully charged and updated iPad is a must.)

Cultivating Communication in the Classroom

How can secondary teachers better prepare their students for an unknown future? How can oral, written, visual, and nonverbal communication skills be nurtured? How do we ensure that our communications are conveyed appropriately? And how do we support conflict resolution, problem solving, empathy, critical thinking, and self-advocacy with any tool we select? Discover the secrets to cultivate communication in your classroom using a wide range of activities from email etiquette and positive interdependence to critical evaluation and creation of social media, curation, and digital portfolios that put students' best feet forward.

Managing Your Digital Life

This highly interactive session highlights both analog and digital strategies for secondary students to set goals, dissolve distractions, manage time, and create healthy habits. Participants will explore five stations that provide firsthand experience with a variety of tools and best practices. Participants will also have time to engage in thoughtful conversations around these ideas and strategies. This session is thoroughly researched and includes practical ideas and applications from students and industry experts. Let's dial up the productivity, dial down the distraction, and get on track for college and career success!

Notable Note-Taking

Do you lose things in Evernote and Google Docs? Do you lament when you can't sketchnote with actual pens, paper, and washi tape? Do you need a better way to organize your thoughts and ideas? This session is for you. This session will highlight strategies that blend analog and digital notes when taking notes in lectures and PD or reading and journaling. Let's go analog and learn how to life and productivity hack your note-taking practices. But wait! there's more . . . you can take the analog and digitize it too! Bring your pens, paper, and iPad and dive into the world of notable note-taking!

Shaping Slides for Saturation

Most educators use a slide deck at some point. Are your slides stagnant, or do they leave your audience spellbound and eager to share? Join in this fast-paced session interspersed with thought-provoking dialogues to level up how you communicate with visuals and your own content. We will blend research-based strategies, tips for organizing content, and designing slides (*including theme, template, and layout*) using images, color, and data, and delivering memorable presentations. This savory session will culminate with a toolkit of support resources including an infographic, curated research and examples, and a list of tools that can support you with both design and appropriate use of creative commons images. You will find that Shaping Slides feeds your hunger for both compelling content and inspiration for irresistible ways to be your own digital architect.

Surprisingly Educational Books for the Classroom

Why talk about books at a convention for educators and technology? In a world of rapid and ephemeral communication and pings, books hold so much interrupted, grounded content, pedagogy, and research. Too often we dismiss them for a quick Google search or a nugget of an article in a tweet. This session is a deep-dive tour through a lovely list of educational books that can impact your daily personal and professional life today! Learn how artists, poets, CEO's, and NY Times Bestselling authors can teach us the necessary skills we need to excel in the world of Ed Tech. You won't want to miss this crafty, carefully curated collection!

Three Strategies for an Instructional Design Reboot

We expect our students to communicate clearly and effectively during projects and publishing. Communication skills and instructions are fostered and delivered not only through our oral directions but the written communications and instructional materials that we provide to our students. How can we use best practices and model effective communication strategies to ensure that our students not only understand what is expected of them but can carefully execute an assignment without confusion or need for constant clarity? This three-part strategy of chunking information, providing visual cues, revising text, and formatting is a tried-and-true practice that has been developed through research-based strategies and honed through actual student classroom encounters. Don't miss Three Fantastic Strategies for Kick Starting and Doctoring Your Instructional Designs.

For more information and to see testimonials, visit

🌐 techchef4u.com/speaking

To find out more about some of the titles listed above, visit

🌐 techchef4u.com/portfolio

Connect with Lisa Johnson

✉️ techchef4u@gmail.com

🐦 @TechChef4u

📘 @TechChef4u

📷 @NoteChef4u

📌 @TechChef4u

THE TECHCHEF4U STORY

TechChef4u (techchef4u.com) was created back in May of 2011. I had recently received my first iPad and was searching the web and edusphere for apps and ideas on how to use it. I had also taken my first job as a full-time Instructional Technologist. I was looking for a tool to share my own ideas and iPad Lessons in an organized fashion. At the time, we had teacher websites that were not conducive to organization and easy location of resources. If I ever left the district, all the resources I had created and curated would be wiped away, and the site would be shut down for everyone benefitting from it within and beyond the district. So I decided to start a "rogue" WordPress site to share ideas, blog posts, iPad Lessons, etc. I also decided to use Pinterest (which was in invitation only at the time) as a way to curate the iPad Lesson ideas I found from people all over the world.

Fast-forward to 2018: I have written/authored over three hundred blog posts on the techchef4u.com site, and a quick Google search for "iPad Lessons" will locate my Pinterest boards as one of the first hits in the list. Those boards now hold more than just iPad Lessons; close to one hundred boards and almost fifteen thousand pins share Book Creation "App-tivities" and Collage/Comic App-tivities. Also shared are Social Emotional Learning, Books that Ignite Literacy, Organization and Journaling, and much more.

I devote a lot of time to creating and curating vetted ideas and resources for others. And that is really where the TechChef4u philosophy came from. I have a Master's in Curriculum and Instruction and have loved writing curriculum and designing learning experiences for others for over a decade. I could have called myself the iPadChef, but I felt like technologies would continue to evolve as the years march on. After all, technology is really just the development and use of simple tools. These tools could be fire, a telephone, a graphing calculator, a pencil, or an iPad, to name a few. TechChef4u doesn't represent a single tool, product, or process but essentially a proactive, purposeful, and positive attitude towards life and learning. The heart of TechChef4u is basically that . . . to create and curate quality recipes with vetted ingredients and a variety of tools . . . for others.

Every few years, I do a value audit (mentioned in Chapter 4). Whatever your career or stage in life, I highly suggest this process. Some of the values that resonated with me were credibility, enthusiasm, inspiration, making a difference, uniqueness, simplicity, and playfulness. Just like this book focuses on dualities, TechChef4u does too. I don't just create; I curate too. I share both analog and digital tools and processes. I am both an author and a reader, a learner and a leader. I keep these ideas and ideals close to my heart when I craft content for public consumption. They are my teaching, learning, and leading philosophy in a nutshell. And just like I keep them at the forefront of my mind when I blog and post on social media, they were at the forefront of my mind when I wrote this book.

ACKNOWLEDGMENTS

This book has been a journey. And this journey would not have been possible without the support of my family and friends. Many thanks to the initial reviewers of this book, Tami Brewster, Brianna Hodges, Mia Morrison, Zandra Lopez, Jennifer Williams—your willingness to help a friend with a very short deadline means so much to me. I also want to thank all of my fellow colleagues who were gracious enough to share their innovative ideas: Beth Keith, Susanna McConnell, Jackie Compean, Allyson White, Ashley Baker, Debbie Smith, and Kacy Williams.

I'm sending a big shout to my Instagram family. Many of you didn't even know me and were kind of enough to respond to my relentless emails and direct messages for permissions to use your work to impact students and educators all around the globe.

I am eternally grateful to my twenty-three amazing contributors who gave freely of their time and insight to make the Working Wisdoms a treasure trove of wisdom: Reshan Richards, Judy Jacomino, Mary Johnson, Efraín E. Vélez, Peter Nevland, Jacob Hanson, Dan Kemp, Danny Johnson, Audrey O'Clair, Cynthia Perkins, Chelle Neff, Demetrius Lewis, Deb Evans, Whitney Woodard, Bria Jones, Manish Kothari, Andrew Gardner, Michael Crawford, Sabina Bharwani, Melissa Johnson, Kayla Cagan, and James Burke.

Thank you to Erin Casey and her team at My Writers' Connection for their craft and your care in removing my overuse of ellipses, smoothing out my thoughts and feelings and making this book beautiful. Genesis Kohler, you are a master at cover design and you absolutely brought this book to life with your graphics and attention to detail.

And finally, thank you to the entire Dave Burgess Consulting, Inc. team. This would not have been possible without you.

MORE FROM DAVE BURGESS Consulting, Inc.

Since 2012, DBCI has been publishing books that inspire and equip educators to be their best. For more information on our DBCI titles or to purchase bulk orders for your school, district, or book study, visit **DaveBurgessconsulting.com/DBCIbooks**.

More from the *PIRATE*™ Series

Teach Like a PIRATE by Dave Burgess
eXPlore Like a Pirate by Michael Matera
Learn Like a Pirate by Paul Solarz
Play Like a Pirate by Quinn Rollins
Run Like a Pirate by Adam Welcome

***Lead Like a PIRATE*™ Series**

Lead Like a PIRATE by Shelley Burgess and Beth Houf
Balance Like a Pirate by Jessica Cabeen, Jessica Johnson, and
  Sarah Johnson
Lead with Culture by Jay Billy
Lead with Literacy by Mandy Ellis

Leadership & School Culture

Culturize by Jimmy Casas
Escaping the School Leader's Dunk Tank by Rebecca Coda and
  Rick Jetter
The Innovator's Mindset by George Couros

Kids Deserve It! by Todd Nesloney and Adam Welcome
Let Them Speak by Rebecca Coda and Rick Jetter
The Limitless School by Abe Hege and Adam Dovico
The Pepper Effect by Sean Gaillard
The Principled Principal by Jeffrey Zoul and Anthony McConnell
The Secret Solution by Todd Whitaker, Sam Miller, and Ryan Donlan
Start. Right. Now. by Todd Whitaker, Jeffrey Zoul, and Jimmy Casas
Stop. Right. Now. by Jimmy Casas and Jeffrey Zoul
Unmapped Potential by Julie Hasson and Missy Lennard
Your School Rocks by Ryan McLane and Eric Lowe

Technology & Tools

50 Things You Can Do with Google Classroom by Alice Keeler and Libbi Miller
50 Things to Go Further with Google Classroom by Alice Keeler and Libbi Miller
140 Twitter Tips for Educators by Brad Currie, Billy Krakower, and Scott Rocco
Code Breaker by Brian Aspinall
Google Apps for Littles by Christine Pinto and Alice Keeler
Master the Media by Julie Smith
Shake Up Learning by Kasey Bell
Social LEADia by Jennifer Casa-Todd
Teaching Math with Google Apps by Alice Keeler and Diana Herrington

Teaching Methods & Materials

All 4s and 5s by Andrew Sharos
Ditch That Homework by Matt Miller and Alice Keeler
Ditch That Textbook by Matt Miller
The EduProtocol Field Guide by Marlena Hebern and Jon Corippo
Instant Relevance by Denis Sheeran
LAUNCH by John Spencer and A.J. Juliani
Make Learning MAGICAL by Tisha Richmond

Pure Genius by Don Wettrick
Shift This! by Joy Kirr
Spark Learning by Ramsey Musallam
Sparks in the Dark by Travis Crowder and Todd Nesloney
Table Talk Math by John Stevens
The Classroom Chef by John Stevens and Matt Vaudrey
The Wild Card by Hope and Wade King
The Writing on the Classroom Wall by Steve Wyborney

Inspiration, Professional Growth & Personal Development
The Four O'Clock Faculty by Rich Czyz
Be REAL by Tara Martin
Be the One for Kids by Ryan Sheehy
The EduNinja Mindset by Jennifer Burdis
How Much Water do We Have? by Pete and Kris Nunweiler
P Is for Pirate by Dave and Shelley Burgess
The Path to Serendipity by Allyson Aspey
Sanctuaries by Dan Tricarico
Shattering the Perfect Teacher Myth by Aaron Hogan
Stories from Webb by Todd Nesloney
Talk to Me by Kim Bearden
The Zen Teacher by Dan Tricarico

Children's Books
Dolphins in Trees by Aaron Polansky
The Princes of Serendip by Allyson Apsey

ABOUT THE AUTHOR

This book is meant to be a love letter and a guidebook to the perennial, to things that matter, have mattered, and will continue to matter. This book is also deeply personal, as I share many of my own insights, projects, processes, and stories. To stay true to this theme, I thought I would hack the old author biography a bit. Sure, biographies are perennial, but they do evolve and grow in different ways. And as this book has a firm foundation in journaling and reflection, I thought you might appreciate the baker's dozen of questions and answers:

Have you lived in any other states other than Texas (where you currently reside)? Yes: Florida, Pennsylvania, and Tennessee.

What is your favorite book? Hands down, the Outlander series. I have adored Diana Gabaldon, Claire, and Jamie for twenty years

What is something not everyone knows about you? Most people know that I love Blue October. Few people know that I was actually in their music video for "The Chills," which was filmed in San Marcos, Texas.

If you could eat only one food for the rest of your life, what would it be? I love me some gnocchi.

What is your favorite planner? I really do love the Passion Planner. I have bought one for the past three years.

What songs from high school totally take you back? "Lightning Crashes" by Live, anything by Collective Soul, and "Glycerine" by Bush.

What are your favorite pens for taking notes? I love the Sharpie Art Pens Fine Point and Faber Castell Pitt Artist Brush Pens. When I get them, I organize them in ROYGBIV order for my own sanity.

What are your favorite Netflix series? *On My Block, Friends, Love, Ozark, Stranger Things, The Crown, Jane the Virgin, Grace and Frankie,* and *Fuller House.* (See, I wasn't joking about the binge-watching and procrastination.)

What are the names of your pets? I named all our pets after characters in movies. Falkor (RIP) was named after the flying dog in *The Neverending Story,* Lanie was named after the main character in the 80s romantic comedy *Dream a Little Dream,* and Cullen was named after the shiny vampire family from the *Twilight* series.

What does a typical day at work look like? I am an Educational Technologist at a 1:1 high school. No day is ever the same, and I absolutely love that about my job. I also love working directly with students as well as staff. One day I will be in meetings and working with professional learning communities. Another day I will be teaching visual literacy and slide design to students developing pitch decks in our incubator class. Another day I will be troubleshooting video projects in English classes right before I deliver a webinar for parents on digital distractions and time management.

What is your favorite color? Anything teal, turquoise, cerulean, and cyan.

What are your favorite professional development conferences? I have been very fortunate to attend and present at a variety of conferences all over the nation and the globe. My favorites to date (based on the caliber of speakers and content gleaned) are Learning and the Brain, Corwin's Women in Leadership, Texas Library Association, and SXSWEDU. And totally not necessarily under the educational umbrella, but the Wild for Planners conference was straight-up legit amazing! I also highly encourage you to attend events that are not necessarily designed for educators but could definitely provide college and career ready insight. I am pretty sure I was the only educator that attended the inaugural On the Dot See it to Be it Success Summit and the nuggets I gleaned from politicians, entrepreneurial women, certified forensic interviewers, and Diversity and Inclusion leaders were invaluable.

If money weren't an option and you could have any other job than your current one, what would you do? Honestly, I have loved to write since I was a small child, so I would continue to do that. My latent passion would be to have my own line of planners, stickers, etc. at Michael's.

To learn more about Lisa Johnson, visit

🌐 techchef4u.com/speaking

To find out more about the myriad of resources
she has authored and curated, visit

🌐 techchef4u.com/portfolio

And don't forget to hit up techchef4u.com/book
as new resources for the book will be added.

Connect with Lisa Johnson

✉️ techchef4u@gmail.com

🐦 @TechChef4u

📘 @TechChef4u

📷 @NoteChef4u

📌 @TechChef4u

CPSIA information can be obtained
at www.ICGtesting.com
Printed in the USA
LVHW021922210119
604682LV00019B/776